Personalize

Personalize

Meeting the Needs of All Learners

Eric Sheninger

Nicki Slaugh

ConnectEDD Publishing
Hanover, Pennsylvania

This publication is available at discount pricing when purchased in quantity for educational purposes, promotions, or fundraisers. For inquiries and details, contact the publisher at: info@connecteddpublishing.com

Published by ConnectEDD Publishing LLC
Hanover, PA
www.connecteddpublishing.com

Cover Design: Kheila Casas

Personalize by Eric Sheninger and Nicki Slaugh. —1st ed. Paperback
ISBN 979-8-9890027-3-3

Praise for *Personalize*

Personalization requires teamwork, risk-taking, a depth and range of teaching strategies, openness to feedback, proof that your teaching is making learning happen, sharing what success looks like, listening to self and students, and a relentless focus on how each student is learning, their beliefs, emotions, and life stories. Personalization is hard work, but Sheninger and Slaugh are right—it is the right work, and this book will make it more understandable, doable, and enjoyable.

—John Hattie | Melbourne Laureate Professor Emeritus

This book is needed right now! Too many teachers are exhausted and leaving this profession, and too many students are not engaged or invested in learning. These are symptoms of a larger problem. In a world where information is easily accessible online, educators must reimagine their roles, shifting from experts at the front of the class to facilitators working alongside learners. Eric Sheninger and Nicki Slaugh present a path forward that prioritizes a dynamic partnership between teacher and learner, ensuring students develop the skills needed to thrive in a rapidly changing world. Instead of seeing the beautifully diverse groups of students in our classrooms as problematic, educators must cultivate instructional strategies to personalize the learning experience, ensuring each student gets what they need to learn and grow. This book is a must-read for any educator frustrated with the status quo, seeking to reignite their passion for teaching, and committed to creating more equitable learning environments where every student can succeed.

—Catlin R. Tucker, Ed.D. | Educator, International Trainer,
Keynote Speaker & Bestselling Author

I am particularly excited about the prospects for this book. The title alone, *Personalize: Meeting the Needs of All Learners*, speaks to my "education soul." Children do not learn alike, and they are not of the same cultural, socio-economic, or experiential backgrounds which all factor into readiness. *Personalize* makes it very clear that if students are going to be able to enjoy the benefits of a quality education, instruction must be crafted in a way that meets their specific learning needs toward meeting the children where they are and as they are.

—Principal Baruti Kafele | Retired Principal, Education
    Consultant, Author

Eric Sheninger and Nicki Slaugh have created a resource that truly lays out the goal of meeting the needs of all learners. What makes this book special is that it is packed with useful suggestions and practical strategies aligned with research and high-agency approaches. Educators looking to achieve greater learning for every student will find it here.

—Jim Knight | Founder and Senior Partner of Instructional
    Coaching Group (ICG)

A gifted guide in helping educators forge their way, Sheninger and Slaugh shed light on how to transform schools into inspired places igniting the interests and expanding the possibilities for our learners. *Personalize: Meeting the Needs of All Learners* makes a clear case for shifting the culture of teaching and the structure of school programs to be responsive to learning and learners. Not only do they demonstrate the need, but they provide clear, beautifully organized strategies that are actionable. Their work is remarkably adaptive for any school environment wishing to partner with learners in preparing them for their future.

—Heidi Hayes Jacobs | Author, Consultant, Curriculum and School
    Designer

Personalize is a powerful and transformative exploration of learning to meet the needs of individual students. Eric and Nicki eloquently challenge the traditional, one-size-fits-all approach, advocating for a dynamic, student-centered model that celebrates everyone's distinctive characteristics. This book is an essential guide for educators ready to embrace change, offering practical strategies and inspiring examples to create engaging, effective learning environments tailored to each student.

> —Winston Y. Sakurai, Ed.D. | Curriculum Innovation Branch Director Hawaii State Department of Education

Personalize: Meeting the Needs of All Learners is a reader-friendly guide filled with practical and easy-to-implement ideas that will help serve as a catalyst for maximum change in today's classrooms. Sheninger and Slaugh offer succinct ideas and explorations of how to increase and honor student voice and choice in the classroom for all learners. A great manual for looking at how to begin making positive cultural and pedagogical changes within any learning environment.

> —Adam Bellow | Co-founder and CEO, Breakout EDU

Personalized learning can feel overwhelming, but Eric Sheninger and Nicki Slaugh break it down with clarity and actionable steps. This book isn't just about theory; it addresses educators' common challenges and provides clear solutions and strategies to overcome them. From tips for station rotation to strategies to elevate co-teaching, it's full of ideas you can implement immediately. Packed with real-world classroom examples and inspiring educator stories, this is a must-read for anyone ready to make personalized learning a reality in their classroom.

> —Monica Burns, Ed.D. | author of *EdTech Essentials*

Eric and Nicki have put together a practical approach to personalizing learning that goes beyond a simple collection of words. *Personalize* is a powerful guide for transforming education through student agency. The book provides educators with a clear roadmap, with specific examples and narratives to tailor learning experiences to meet the needs of each and every learner.

—Ken Shelton | International Speaker, Consult, and Founder of Elevate Education

Personalize: Meeting the Needs of All Learners is a transformative guide for educators seeking to break free from traditional teaching models. Sheninger and Slaugh masterfully blend theory and practice, offering actionable steps to personalize instruction and enhance student agency while building meaningful relationships. With useable strategies, evidence-based practices, and inspiring insights, each chapter empowers educators to create engaging learner-centered experiences and environments. This book is a must-read for any educator committed to enhancing each learner's unique passions, interests, and abilities!

—Thomas C. Murray | Director of Innovation, Future Ready Schools Best Selling Author

Timely and relevant, Eric Sheninger and Nicki Slaugh manage to target the crux of the matter. While we acknowledge the need for hyper-personalization for our students, it isn't always easy for teachers who take pride in meticulously planning their lessons. What is exciting is that the educational ecosystem is lending itself to action research in real time! Eric and Nicki's work takes them around the world directing, adapting, and even educating school teams globally. Their engagement and writing are like a breath of fresh air for teachers and leadership teams alike, as it endorses the work being done in progressive schools and yet offers tweaks that enhance what is already in place. When the lines between pedagogical approaches and the use of educational technology begin to blur, you know that the learning for students will be at a rarified level.

—Nargish Khambatta | Principal and Senior Vice President of Education, GEMS

Eric Sheninger and Nicki Slaugh's *Personalize* is an essential guide for educators striving to create inclusive and dynamic learning environments. The book's exploration of the importance of culture, empowering students through agency, meeting diverse needs, and prioritizing relationships offers invaluable insights and practical strategies. Their wisdom on cultivating a positive school culture and fostering meaningful relationships is particularly compelling. This book is a must-read for any educator dedicated to enhancing student engagement and improving student outcomes.

—LaTonya Goffney | Superintendent, Aldine Independent School District

The "vibe" matters as teachers nurture the learner's journey, blending deep personal experiences and curated collaborations. Eric Sheninger and Nicki Slaugh recognize the need for this key perspective, which unlocks student agency and delivers their futures.

—Kirk Koennecke | Superintendent, Indian Hill Exempted Village School District

Slaugh and Sheninger offer a fantastic resource for all educators to provide opportunities for personalization at every level of a school. They know and understand that learning is not isolated to students, and they do a great job of connecting ownership to learning for everyone in a building. The *Bold Moves* in each chapter give you ideas to put in place immediately while not overwhelming those you lead. This is definitely a book teachers, administrators, and coaches will want on their shelves.

—Joe Sanfelippo, PhD. | Author, Speaker

I am excited about this book! The customization and personalization of Nicki Slaugh's school is impressive and has me telling everyone I know! And Eric Sheninger has been a go-to education guru for many years. I am excited about this collaboration and know that it will be useful to all of us as we move forward into an era of collaboration and personalization. It can be done! It is already happening! This book will show us all how.

—Vicki Davis | Cool Cat Teacher Blog, 10 Minute Teacher Podcast

Eric Sheninger's undeniable expertise in blended and personalized learning shines in his latest collaboration with practitioner Nicki Slaugh. Together, they offer educators a book that is as relevant as it is inspiring. Personalize pushes each of us to be BOLD in our pursuit of joyful, engaging, and personalized learning that meets the needs of all students, regardless of zip code.

—Weston Kieschnick | International Speaker/Best-Selling Author/ Coach

We will never get to *all* until we reach *each*. For some reason and for far too long, we have seemed to miss this point in our profession with our mind-numbingly-mad adherence to the all-learn-in-the-same-way-and-time approach to education. One size does not—*cannot*—fit all. Intuitively, we know this, but our knowing has not led to our doing. And, as such, we stay stuck in our striving for (but never reaching) all. It's time (past time) to reach each. And now, at long last, there's hope. This book gives me hope for the each we teach. From the philosophical foundation to the practical application of a personalized approach for meeting the needs of each human in the room, Eric and Nicki have delivered the right book at the right time. Indeed, this book will help us all brave and build a better education for *each* of our kids.

—Monte Syrie | HS ELA teacher and author of *better: A Teacher's Journey.*

Sheninger's expertise as a global thought leader, combined with Slaugh's hands-on experience as a middle school principal, results in this extremely accessible guide that bridges theory and practice for educators eager to delve into personalized learning. This book provides a rich resource for school leaders and teachers, offering a well-researched and evidence-based exploration of personalization and learner agency. The authors skillfully translate complex concepts into practical models and frameworks enriched with vivid, real-world examples. This compelling blend of insights and actionable strategies makes it an indispensable resource for anyone committed to transforming their classroom through personalized learning.

> —Derek Wenmoth | Founder, FutureMakers and Author, Agency By Design: An Educator's Playbook

Personalize: Meeting the Needs of All Learners is designed to empower educators with the tools and knowledge necessary to create a positive and inclusive classroom culture. It equips all educators with the skills to adapt their teaching methods to maximize student engagement and opportunities for success. Nicki and Eric provide practical insights and strategies that can truly transform education experiences into a more personalized approach for every student. I have witnessed their work and attest it can make a difference in ensuring that all students have the opportunities to succeed.

> —Sydnee Dickson, Ed.D. | State Superintendent of Public Instruction, Utah State Board of Education

Eric Sheninger and Nicki Slaugh emphasize the crucial need for educators to transition from the traditional factory education model to personalized and individualized learning. They go beyond theory and focus on practical, actionable, and achievable solutions from educators creating a classroom culture focused on student-centric learning. They assert themselves as thought leaders in educational transformation because they dedicate quality time to where the action is: the classroom.

—Dwight Carter | Director of Student Support Systems, Author, Speaker

Nicki Slaugh and Eric Sheninger have hit it out of the park with *Personalize*. This is one of those books filled with innovative and challenging ideas, and I continually found myself reflecting on my work and how I can be better. I love how you can read the book cover to cover or just pick it up when and where you need to! This book will be one that I share (and come back to myself) for many years to come.

—Todd Nesloney | Director of Culture and Strategic Leadership, TEPSA

Personalize is what is needed now more than ever! If you are an educator who knows how invaluable commitment to innovation and growth are, then you know this is an essential read for educators. By prioritizing the LEARNER over the content, Eric and Nicki pave the way for a more effective and personal educational experience for both students and teachers. This book is the one!

—LaVonna Roth | Founder of Ignite Your S.H.I.N.E, keynote speaker

Table of Contents

Introduction

Growing up in rural Idaho in the 1980s, my school days were marked by a lack of personalization. As a middle school student, I breezed through new concepts, leaving me with ample idle time during class. Predictably, this boredom led to chatting with friends, disrupting classmates, and frustrating teachers. The recurring cycle of being "invited" to the hall seemed unbreakable until my freshman year of high school.

Enter an extraordinary English teacher, nearing retirement but light years ahead in her approach to teaching. Unlike previous teachers, she did not attempt to coerce compliance but chose instead to challenge me. She introduced me to The Iliad by Homer, proposing a daily reading routine and weekly writings. I embraced the challenge wholeheartedly, reading it during class and immersing myself in the Ancient Greek epic at home. This teacher understood the importance of engaging students at their levels, a revelation in a system not inherently designed for such tailored approaches. Throughout high school, she continued to introduce me to challenging texts, sparking a lifelong love for learning through reading.

Fast-forward several years, and now, as an educator, I grapple with the limitations of traditional teaching methods. Despite using station rotations and small group instruction, some students were bored and not reaching their full potential, while others needed help keeping pace with the class. At this juncture, my principal, Nicki

1

Slaugh, challenged me to implement self-paced learning in my math classes.

Reflecting on my 9th-grade English teacher's impact on my life, I accepted the challenge. Collaborating with other teachers and experimenting with self-pacing, we fine-tuned our approach over the next few years. Today, our blended learning environment at Quest Academy Junior High School combines online and teacher-led learning, empowering students to progress at their own pace. Real-time data and regular conferences with the teacher determine the needed instruction and practice level, personalizing each student's learning pathway. When students feel confident in mastering a standard, they take the assessment and seamlessly move on to the next one.

This intentional blend eliminates the boredom of busy work and the frustration of struggling to grasp a concept without sufficient time and practice. As an educator, the satisfaction of meeting the needs of my students is immeasurable. After several years in this self-paced environment, returning to traditional methods seems unimaginable. Tailoring instruction to each student precisely when they are ready to learn is not just rewarding but has a lasting impact, much like the transformative influence my English teacher had on me years ago.

—Mary Trujillo, 6th Grade Teacher

This is the crux of the challenge facing modern education. Classrooms brimming with curious learners are often trapped in a system built on uniformity. Mary's story exemplifies a pressing need to evolve. Change, however, can be daunting. We usually teach as we were taught, perpetuating traditional methods out of habit or comfort. This book is a call to action, a challenge to break free from the shackles of "That's the way we've always done it." The traditional model operates under the false assumption that all students learn at the same pace and in the same way. This fallacy leads to frustration, boredom, and disengagement. Effective learning hinges on recognizing the unique abilities and interests each student brings to the classroom.

> Effective learning hinges on recognizing the unique abilities and interests each student brings to the classroom.

While some may resist change, clinging to the familiar, growth demands reevaluation. Shifting our focus from simply *delivering instruction* to *nurturing student learning* is critical. The instruction tells, learning shows (Sheninger, 2021). Personalization prioritizes the "who" (the learner) over the "what" (content). This book dives into the transformative power of personalization. It is a move away from impersonal, one-size-fits-all approaches that leave many students behind. Personalized learning ensures all students get what they need when they need it, fostering a sense of ownership over the learning process. It is a move from a curriculum-centered approach to student-centered learning, where knowledge is acquired and applied to real-world problems.

Creating a thriving culture is imperative if we are to achieve our goals. We set out to define this culture as a dynamic educational environment that recognizes and celebrates the uniqueness of each learner. It fosters curiosity, critical thinking, and creativity by tailoring learning experiences to individual interests, strengths, and aspirations. In this culture, learners actively co-create knowledge, collaborate, and explore diverse perspectives, empowering them to thrive in an ever-evolving world. The role of the educator is critical in making this a reality, and we will unpack the many dispositions, shifts to practice, and support needed to lead to a culture of learning in which personalization flourishes.

The benefits of personalization are far-reaching. Students gain a deeper understanding of subjects, develop critical thinking skills, and build on their strengths. Personalized learning encourages independence and self-regulation, empowering students to become self-directed learners. Various learning strategies, like offering students voice, choice, path, pace, and place cater to needs and learning preferences. Additionally, personalization seamlessly aligns with intervention systems, ensuring targeted support for students who need it most.

Technology can be a powerful tool to support personalization, but it is essential to remember that pedagogy reigns supreme. The priority remains to create equitable learning experiences—ensuring *every* student can thrive. The current educational model often leads to a lopsided learning environment prioritizing rote memorization over critical thinking. Surface-level assessments focusing on ease of grading fail to capture a student's proper understanding of content. A score of 15/20 on a science quiz—what does it tell us? Are students simply regurgitating information or developing the critical skills to solve complex problems? This overreliance on shallow assessments wastes valuable time and hinders our ability to collect meaningful data about student progress. Teachers burdened by such tasks often face burnout, feeling their work lacks purpose.

In its earlier forms, education relied heavily on one-way lectures, a model ripe for disengagement. Students became passive participants, compliant rather than engaged. The focus changed from genuine learning to accumulating points, turning education into a game. Additionally, educators across the globe express fatigue and a sense of disconnect due to student disengagement. This negativity permeates the learning environment, impacting student achievement. Shifting away from traditional practices can rekindle the passion educators once felt. Personalized learning models offer renewed meaning and purpose, transforming classrooms into dynamic hubs of exploration and discovery.

This book is structured so that educators can either read from cover to cover or choose a particular chapter that is of specific interest or represents a needed opportunity for growth. We did this because there is no right or best way to personalize, and we would never assume that facets of personalization are not currently taking place. Just like for our learners, the reader should be empowered to follow their path based on interests and needs. Each chapter is supported by research, practical strategies, and anecdotal stories for essential context. At the end, there is a summary section titled "Bold Moves." These are courageous decisions that break away from traditional methods and push boundaries. They involve calculated risks and innovative solutions to address challenges and empower student growth through personalization. The questions in these sections are meant to inspire bold actions.

Readers will also find embedded examples of personalized strategies to illustrate how this can work in classrooms. This is further supported by a digital appendix that fleshes out not only how to effectively personalize but also what it could look like across various grade levels and content areas. Get ready to see and hear what personalization can look and feel like when implemented with fidelity. However, while we share concepts we strongly believe in and that have worked for many educators, it is essential to understand that for others, this will not solve all problems.

Think back to Mary's story. Her thirst for knowledge went unaddressed in her traditional middle school classes, leading to disengagement. Personalized learning, exemplified by her exceptional English teacher, provided her with a challenge that matched her abilities, igniting a love for learning that continues today. As an educator, Mary recognized the limitations of one-size-fits-all methods. By implementing self-paced learning, she created an environment in which students could progress at their speed both those who grasped concepts quickly and those who needed more time. This catered to individual needs and maximized student potential. We hope this book impacts you in the same way that Mary's teacher impacted her.

Let's take a collective leap of faith and move from traditional instruction to personalization. By adapting practices to each student when appropriate, we can make learning relevant, engaging, and, most importantly, effective. In this new paradigm, educators like Mary can finally find their niche, and their spark of curiosity fanned into a life-long love of teaching and learning.

CHAPTER 1

The Importance
of Culture

G reenview School is a rural institution that has stood for over a century. Its weathered stone walls whisper tales of a bygone era, echoing the school's long-held emphasis on discipline and academic rigor. Greenview boasts a reputation for excellence, but some might say its environment is as cold and unforgiving as the stone from which it is built.

The town reflects a similar stoicism, its tranquility starkly contrasting the competitive atmosphere within Greenview's halls. Here, we meet Janice, a bright-eyed young student whose curiosity and enthusiasm for life break the mold. Janice believes in the power of creativity, kindness, and joy—values she finds sorely lacking in her academic environment. While her classmates excel at achieving top marks, Janice longs for a more holistic education characteristic of well-rounded individuals.

A new season arrives at Greenview, not just in the changing leaves but with the appointment of a new principal, Mr. Hawthorne. A man of uncommon vision, Mr. Hawthorne possesses a gentle smile and a philosophy far beyond textbooks and test scores. He recognizes the potential for something more significant within the hallowed halls of Greenview and sets his sights on cultivating a transformed school culture.

Mr. Hawthorne's approach is unconventional. He introduces the "Orchard of Wisdom," a unique concept that serves as both a symbolic and physical space for students to learn and grow beyond the confines of the traditional classroom. Planted with various trees, each symbolizing a core value such as compassion, resilience, and collaboration, the orchard becomes a student-led haven where they nurture the trees and the values they represent.

As the orchard flourishes, so too do the students. Janice enthusiastically takes to the project, becoming a leading gardener in the Orchard of Wisdom. Under Mr. Hawthorne's guidance, a metamorphosis begins to take root within Greenview. Classrooms transform into interactive spaces where rote memorization gives way to critical thinking and creative exploration. The arts are placed on equal footing with the sciences, and a spirit of sportsmanship is celebrated alongside academic achievement. Perhaps the most transformative addition is the "Circle of Stories," a weekly forum at which students and teachers share personal experiences that connect to the values cultivated in the orchard. These stories exhibit empathy, understanding, and a sense of community that had been missing for far too long.

Greenview School is on a path of transformation that blends its cherished traditions with a newfound emphasis on creativity, collaboration, and the importance of nurturing the whole child. Hope emerges as the seasons change and the orchard blossoms, promising a brighter future for Greenview and its students.

With the right culture in place, whether in a classroom or school, anything is possible.

An Educator's "Aha" Moment

In the early days of my teaching career, I, Nicki, found myself in a bustling first-grade classroom filled with excitement and enthusiasm. It was my very first week as a teacher, and I was determined to make a positive impact. My first "aha" moment unfolded as I began to get to know each child individually.

It became evident that each student possessed a unique learning preference, academic level, and personality. Some arrived at school without recognizing letters or sounds, while others were already fluent readers. I was handed a "one-size-fits-all" direct instruction curriculum during those first days. It immediately dawned on me that more than this approach would be required. I needed to personalize my instruction for ALL learners, acknowledging that not every child learns the same way or at the same pace.

As I worked to get to know each child, I discovered their interests and passions. I realized the importance of allowing them to read books of their choosing rather than having everyone read the same book. This first aha moment set the course for my teaching philosophy of putting students first, no matter what. Relationships, connections, and learner growth are all non-negotiable in my heart.

Fast forward to eight years ago, during my first week as a secondary school principal. A sense of déjà vu washed over me as I conducted my initial walk-throughs. Rows of desks, students sitting compliantly, teachers delivering content in a one-size-fits-all manner—a scene that mirrored my early teaching days. At that moment, the second aha moment struck. I saw the students all learning the same content simultaneously and in the same way. The system that had differentiated in the younger grades was now pushing students into a one-size-fits-all program in the secondary setting. It was a pattern that stifled individuality and, in many cases, led to students losing interest in our education system.

I knew, right then and there, that a change was imperative. It was time to break away from this monotonous mold. We risked losing our students' enthusiasm and motivation to learn if we continued down this path. I realized that I needed to take a risk and act swiftly. Thus, I embraced change wholeheartedly, not in fragments. I went "all in" to move the school because I believed every student deserved to have their unique needs met, not just specific classes or grades. This unwavering commitment marked the beginning of a new exploration in secondary education.

All my aha moments revolved around a common theme—putting people first to meet their diverse needs, regardless of their role. If we ask educators to do this for students, we must do the same for them. When people are the priority, positivity naturally flourishes, and deeper relationships are forged, unlocking hidden potential. The best schools recognize the value of allowing teachers to specialize in their subjects and students, personalizing the learning experience for all. These principles have been the guiding light, reminding me that when we put people first, we create a world where every individual's uniqueness is celebrated and nurtured.

My journey has been marked by a dedication to effecting change and transforming various aspects of education as a teacher and leader. Along the way, I have learned how to build high-performing teams, turning negative cultures into ones defined by trust and where integrity is a non-negotiable aspect of our pursuit toward achieving strategic goals. It's time to find *your* ah-ha moment, too.

Unleashing the Power of Teamwork

The phrase "Your vibe attracts your tribe" is more than just a motto; it encapsulates the principle that the energy and attitude you project will naturally attract like-minded individuals. The vibes you emit each day significantly influence those around you in your school environment.

Teamwork is at the essence of academic triumph. In our ever-changing and competitive educational landscape, we must nurture collaboration to attain more extraordinary accomplishments. It is equally crucial in workplaces in order to promote a shared vision, facilitate the exchange of practices, and support emotional and professional growth.

Furthermore, teamwork among staff is associated with creating a more cohesive, supportive, and innovative learning environment for students, contributing to a culture of continuous improvement and adaptability within educational settings (Bry & Schneider, 2002; Hattie, 2009; Leithwood & Louis, 2010; Lieberman, 2007).

In schools, the unique and varied skills, experiences, and perspectives of students and staff can merge seamlessly to create a dynamic environment for tackling academic challenges. Each team member (students, teachers, and administrators) brings unique talents, contributing to a comprehensive and well-rounded approach and establishing an atmosphere where ideas flow freely.

Having a leader to guide a vibrant team, a pillar of inspiration who recognizes and celebrates each member's strengths, is crucial. By acknowledging and leveraging these individual talents, the leader ensures that the team operates to its full potential. Morale soars and overall academic performance reaches new heights as each teacher feels valued for their distinctive contributions.

Communication is not a mere exchange of words; it is a symphony of voices, each note contributing to the harmony of a school team. Leaders understand the importance of giving everybody a voice, and recognizing each individual's treasure trove of insights. Leaders should provide teachers with a voice; likewise, teachers should give students a voice. Doing this will strengthen the team and build mutual respect and collaboration. When focusing on teamwork, everyone becomes each other's greatest cheerleaders. This creates a positive and supportive learning environment and forges a strong camaraderie among staff members, resulting in harmonious collaboration.

Recognizing and celebrating successes become the cornerstone of building positivity amongst teachers and students. This reinforces a sense of accomplishment and serves as a source of motivation, propelling the entire school toward further collaborative victories. This common purpose provides direction, ensuring that every effort contributes to the overarching objectives of the student team and the school.

Together, administrators, leaders, teachers, and students should set academic objectives. This will illustrate a shared commitment that fuels a sense of accountability and responsibility among everyone. This collaborative effort provides a framework for measuring progress and success, keeping the school team focused on achieving their collective academic objectives. Empowerment will transform the team into a hub of educational innovation and adaptability as individuals embrace a sense of ownership and responsibility for their studies. Trust and confidence among students, teachers, and administrators build a resilient and dynamic academic team.

A collaborative spirit creates a nurturing environment in which individuals feel supported in their academic growth and development. Remembering that everyone brings unique skills and experiences to the classroom is essential. Embracing continuous learning allows them to benefit from each other's academic expertise, adapt to new challenges, and stay ahead in an ever-evolving educational landscape.

In the words of Helen Keller (1903), "Alone, we can learn so little; together, we can learn so much." "This highlights the idea…" The idea is that individuals have limited knowledge or learning capacity when working in isolation. However, when people collaborate and work together, their collective efforts, insights, and experiences lead to a significantly more profound understanding. Creating a team environment can lead to collaboration, innovation, and a sense of shared purpose, ultimately leading to improved outcomes and a more positive and fulfilling experience for the individuals involved.

The Role of Risk-Taking

To be a trailblazer in reshaping the educational experience, one must embark on an expedition that involves a willingness to take risks, challenge the status quo, and innovate with a purpose. Transforming a classroom requires visionary educators who understand that the path to progress is often paved with bold decisions and calculated risks.

Risk-taking in education is not about recklessness; instead, it is about having the courage to question established norms and explore uncharted territories in pursuit of a better learning environment. Ask yourself, are you naturally curious? Do you ask "Why?" or "How?" about various aspects of life, systems, or ideas? Are you open-minded? If so, we encourage you to try something new that will uncover a world of possibilities.

At the heart of any transformation is visionary leadership. Educators who dare to dream beyond conventional boundaries are more likely to initiate changes that lead to meaningful impact. A willingness to take risks in implementing new teaching methodologies, revising curricula, and adopting innovative technologies is crucial for creating a forward-thinking environment. Personalized learning is just that: breaking away from the one-size-fits-all approach to help all students succeed.

> **Personalized learning is just that: breaking away from the one-size-fits-all approach to help all students succeed.**

Transformation is inherently disruptive, and introducing change often encounters resistance. Educational trailblazers understand the importance of overcoming the fear of the unknown. Whether introducing project-based learning, integrating technology in the classroom, allowing students to move at their own pace, giving students voice and choice, or revamping assessment methods, the willingness to embrace change is a catalyst for progress.

A transformative educator recognizes that innovation thrives in an environment encouraging experimentation and learning from failure. Building a culture that celebrates creativity, curiosity, and resilience empowers educators and students to explore new ideas and personalized approaches. It creates an atmosphere where taking risks is accepted and encouraged, knowing that failure along with feedback ensure learning and growth.

Risk-taking in education involves prioritizing the needs and aspirations of students. This might entail introducing personalized learning paths, creating interdisciplinary programs, or forging industry partnerships to provide real-world experiences. By tailoring the learning experience, trailblazers ensure that education is not a one-size-fits-all model. Only some risks will yield immediate success; setbacks are inevitable in any transformative endeavor. However, a true trailblazer in education views setbacks as opportunities for learning and improvement. Leaders and educators can turn challenges into steppingstones toward tremendous success by developing a resilient mindset within the school community.

Transforming a classroom or school requires a courageous departure from the familiar. It demands that people take risks, challenge conventions, and envision a system that prepares students for the complexities of the future. As we navigate the uncharted waters of innovation, let us embrace the inherent risks as essential ingredients for creating a learning environment that inspires, challenges, and propels educators and students toward excellence.

Professional Learning

Just as we champion personalized learning experiences for our students, we must also extend the same commitment to developing our teaching workforce. At the heart of this endeavor is recognizing each educator's strengths, areas for growth, aspirations, and professional goals. No two teachers are alike, each with unique strengths, weaknesses, and ambitions. Thus, the cornerstone of professional learning begins with a comprehensive needs assessment. We endeavor to unravel the intricacies of the learning landscape at an individual level through surveys, interviews, or self-assessment tools.

It is the leader's job to do for our teachers what we ask them to do for our students. Provide them with choices and listen to their voice through the thoughtful design of learning plans tailored to each educator's journey. These individualized roadmaps delineate specific learning objectives, activities, and timelines, guiding their quest for professional excellence. When leaders take time to provide them with meaningful and purposeful learning experiences, the relationship between administrators and staff is strengthened.

Leaders need to offer many professional learning avenues, from workshops and conferences to online courses, collaborative projects, and book clubs, allowing educators the autonomy to chart their courses. Within this landscape of choice, we champion the integration of job-embedded learning, seamlessly weaving professional development into the fabric of educators' daily endeavors.

Moreover, take time to recognize the transformative power of collaborative learning communities. Through establishing professional learning communities (PLCs), educators engage in peer-to-peer learning, sharing experiences, resources, and best practices in a nurturing system of collective growth. Mentorship and coaching emerge as support pillars in this personal and professional quest to improve. Each educator is paired with a mentor or coach whose guidance is finely tuned to the individual, promoting personalized support and development.

Leaders should regularly conduct walk-throughs or drop-in visits to all classrooms, which sets a high standard and provides crucial insights for supporting teachers effectively. These visits should be viewed as formative assessments for teachers. During formal evaluations, it is beneficial to video record lessons. Subsequently, the video can be shared with the teacher for self-reflection and self-assessment using an evaluation guide. Following this, a meeting can be scheduled between the teacher and the leader to compare notes. Empowering teachers to critique their performance helps them identify areas for improvement, set goals, and effectively facilitate personal growth.

Technology plays a pivotal role in our quest for personalized learning experiences. Leveraging online platforms and learning management systems, educators engage in self-paced professional development, accessing a wealth of resources tailored to their interests and aspirations.

Furthermore, it is vital to embrace the concept of microlearning, breaking down complex topics into digestible units that fit seamlessly into educators' busy schedules. Regular feedback mechanisms and reflection opportunities guide educators along their learning voyage, enabling them to calibrate their progress and navigate toward continuous improvement.

As stewards of this crusade, leaders celebrate and incentivize educators' commitment to professional development. Recognizing achievements, certifications, and milestones, we fuel the flames of motivation, inspiring collective community growth and excellence. One easy way to accomplish this is by "celebrating success" at the beginning of each faculty meeting. Administrators must provide a time for teachers to reflect on each other's practices, celebrate wins for students, compliment each other, and share what is on their minds.

From an educator's standpoint, continuous refinement of their craft is crucial, coupled with staying current with the latest technological advancements and taking ownership of their learning journey. Remaining steadfast in expectations for students is critical. Here is a specific framework for maximizing the benefits of professional learning:

GUIDE ON HOW TEACHERS CAN UTILIZE PROFESSIONAL LEARNING EFFECTIVELY

Identify Relevant Opportunities

- Research and select professional learning opportunities that directly relate to your goals and teaching context.
- Consider workshops, conferences, online courses, webinars, peer observations, or collaborative projects.

Implement New Strategies

- Integrate newly acquired knowledge and skills into your teaching practice.
- Experiment with different approaches and adapt them to suit your students' needs.

Collaborate and Share

- Collaborate with colleagues to share insights and discuss strategies learned from professional learning.
- Engage in peer observation or coaching sessions to provide and receive feedback.

REMEMBER YOUR GOALS

Set Clear Goals

- Identify specific areas of your teaching practice that you want to improve or develop.
- Define clear, measurable goals that you aim to achieve through professional learning.

Revisit Your Goals

- Periodically revisit your goals and adjust them based on your evolving needs and aspirations.
- Continue to set new challenges and seek opportunities for growth.

Evaluate Effectiveness

- Continuously assess the impact of implemented strategies on student learning outcomes.
- Use assessment data, student feedback, and personal reflections to evaluate effectiveness.

By following these steps, educators can use professional learning opportunities to enhance their personalized teaching practice and benefit students' learning experiences.

Cross-disciplinary learning and long-term career development avenues expand horizons, enriching educators' perspectives and opening doors to leadership roles and specialized training opportunities. With personalization, educators cease to be mere participants; they become architects of their growth, empowered with autonomy and agency in their professional odyssey. Through this holistic approach, leaders and educators will cultivate a vibrant learning culture where the seeds of passion and expertise flourish, enriching their lives and the minds and hearts of their students.

Openness to Feedback

Everyone says they want feedback, but are the people asking for it open to what is being suggested. Here is the connection to creating a learning culture, as defined in the introduction. *Openness to some ideas is critical, as is the facilitation of feedback provided.* Feedback is essential for enhancement in any profession; it is a foundational element for success. Previous discussions have highlighted the crucial nature of receiving quality feedback that offers a comprehensive overview of one's performance, highlighting strengths and pinpointing potential areas for growth or improvement. Such feedback is instrumental in shaping goals and objectives that steer professional development in any given role.

Feedback is pivotal in enhancing performance by acknowledging strengths and providing constructive guidance for improvement. The research underscores that feedback, when effectively delivered, significantly boosts performance across various settings. For instance, Hattie and Timperley (2007) emphasize that effective feedback must answer three critical questions related to the task, the process, and self-regulation, highlighting its role in improving learning outcomes. They argue that such feedback can considerably accelerate student achievement, with their meta-analysis showing a high effect size on learning. Similarly, London and Smither (2002), in their study on feedback orientation, feedback culture, and the longitudinal performance management process, demonstrate that a feedback-rich environment contributes to ongoing employee development and performance enhancement in organizational contexts.

It is critical to differentiate between feedback and criticism. Feedback is constructive information regarding responses to a product or an individual's task performance, which serves as a foundation for progress. Conversely, criticism often entails expressing disapproval based on perceived faults or errors. For the aim of growth, it is pivotal that feedback is presented to encourage reflection and inspire the recipient to engage in actions that lead to improvement.

Feedback's effectiveness hinges not on the giver but on the recipient's perception and assimilation. The essence is to tailor the feedback to resonate well with the receiver. This underscores the importance of focusing as much on the recipient ("who") as on the content of the feedback ("what") to necessitate meaningful growth.

Whether you are a teacher or administrator, growth hinges on quality feedback that people can process. Here are five key aspects to ensure it is constructive and beneficial:

1. **Positive Delivery:** The manner of delivery, including word choice and non-verbal cues, significantly influences the reception of feedback. Blending commendations with areas for growth within a comprehensive development plan can reinforce positive practices while instilling trust and open dialogue.

2. **Practical and Specific:** Feedback should offer immediate actionable advice, ideally supported by research or evidence, to underscore its validity and applicability. Tying feedback to specific learning objectives or professional standards enhances its relevance and utility.

3. **Timeliness:** Prompt feedback is crucial for addressing issues before they escalate and reinforcing positive behaviors when they are most impactful. Delaying feedback diminishes its value and effectiveness.

4. **Consistency:** A steady flow of feedback establishes a supportive and growth-oriented culture. Regular, non-evaluative feedback, such as through learning walks, rubrics, or student portfolios, ensures ongoing development and preparedness for formal evaluations.

5. **Appropriate Medium:** The medium of feedback, influenced by technology, should be chosen based on the context and needs of the recipient. While digital communication is convenient, face-to-face interactions often provide a richer, more personable exchange.

Openness to feedback involves nurturing self-awareness and a proactive attitude toward improvement. Educators can clear up any misunderstandings and gain valuable insights by setting clear personal objectives, actively seeking understanding, and engaging with feedback specifics. Formulating and implementing a targeted action plan based on feedback received showcases a dedication to improving oneself. Moreover, sharing these intentions and soliciting support promotes ongoing advancement. Finally, distinguishing feedback from criticism is vital for its constructive reception. Reflecting on these components can enhance the feedback process, making it a more effective tool for growth and development in a quest to personalize learning.

Celebrate Wins

Building a welcoming, respectful, lifelong learning-oriented school is imperative to the overall success of the school. The primary aim is to cultivate a positivity centered on learning. A simple way to initiate this is through the acknowledgment of achievements. Celebrating accomplishments lifts spirits and sustains a constructive school atmosphere. It promotes ownership of triumphs and propels students and educators alike.

Is there such a thing as a "small" win? We challenge this notion because the overall impact is in the eye of the beholder. Small victories can carry equal or even greater significance than their larger counterparts, and there are two primary reasons for this phenomenon. Without these minor triumphs, attaining significant accomplishments becomes doubtful; we tend to surrender in disappointment and frustration before reaching a grand victory.

These minor successes are the key to maintaining momentum and infusing us with the motivation to persist. Secondly, the grand, enchanting moments we relish occur infrequently. Those monumental breakthroughs are limited in number throughout our lives. This scarcity partly contributes to our profound enjoyment of such moments. Conversely, small wins are more frequent, compensating for their modest size with sheer abundance.

It is human nature to desire to "go big" or make a dramatic change at scale. While we tend to think that this is the ultimate measure of success, the fact is that these situations are few and far between. The challenge then becomes what happens to motivation daily during any change process? Research has shown that small wins are just as important, if not more, than the big ones everyone aspires to achieve. Over four months, Amabile and Kramer (2011) undertook a study involving more than two hundred employees across seven distinct companies. The study's simple daily requirement for participants was to complete an end-of-workday survey, which inquired about their mood, motivation level, and daily work activities. The cumulative outcome of this study amounted to over 12,000 survey responses, all of which underwent subsequent analysis by the research team. It was emphasized that achieving progress in high motivation, engagement, and positive emotions does not necessarily require monumental feats. Accomplishments do not need to be significant breakthroughs as small successes have the potential to leave people with a positive feeling."

The immense value in small wins resides in the immediate impact they can have on an individual and the collective. We have found they also work to:

- Increase motivation.
- Improve morale.
- Provide autonomy.
- Leverage available resources.
- Make the most out of time.
- Serve as a catalyst to learn from problems expeditiously.
- Foster collaboration.

How do you and your school commemorate accomplishments, learning, growth, and mutual support? In a personalized setting where students advance at varying paces and follow tailored pathways, it is beneficial to celebrate learning consistently. This engenders an environment centered on learning, displaying support, and empowering students to excel.

At Nicki's school, teachers incorporate various ways to celebrate success, including students ringing a gong upon demonstrating understanding, broadcasting early completion of grade-level math courses over the intercom, the principal delivering balloons to celebrate learning in classrooms, capturing moments with a Polaroid camera when students reach mastery, adding their name to a glow in the dark star and putting on the ceiling if they pass the assessment the first time, and awarding blue ribbons for exceptional work.

Celebrating achievements should not be limited to students. How does your school celebrate staff accomplishments? Approaches include initiating faculty meetings with triumph celebrations, acknowledging personal and professional achievements, and engaging in "Teachers Supporting Teachers" where staff and teachers each "drop-in" to eight different classrooms during their prep periods taking time to observe and share positive observations via email. These practices enhance school cohesion, forge stronger relationships, and demonstrate mutual support, mitigating teacher burnout—a pressing concern in education.

Healthy competition thrives in positive school atmospheres. It raises standards, nurtures continuous growth, and spurs excellence. Modeling kindness, peer support, constructive feedback, shared celebrations, and high expectations strongly emphasize learning. As students affirm, this environment is transformative.

We must not discount even the most minor successes during good and trying times; doing so is a simple and authentic way to build people up and maintain momentum. Over time, these small wins can morph into catalysts for more extensive change efforts (Sheninger, 2021). In actuality, "small" wins can prove to be huge. Never discount their impact, as they are crucial in setting the stage for bigger ones in the future.

Bold Moves

Education needs champions who work to create a school culture that celebrates personalized learning. At the core, it is tailoring education to individual student needs, abilities, and interests, because this has the power to transform lives. This shift from traditional, one-size-fits-all methods requires educators to embrace flexibility, student empowerment, and technology to individualize learning. Keep in mind the "aha moments" that spark innovation in teaching. These moments highlight the importance of a mindset open to risk-taking and change, all to enrich the learning experience for every student. Personalized learning encourages educators to see and cultivate each student's unique strengths and preferences, which leads to an environment in which all learners can flourish and reach their full potential.

Bold moves require courageous action. These result when we reflect on our practice and determine a more effective path to grow in ways that challenge conventional wisdom or how we were trained. The questions below will help you begin this journey.

1. How can educators move from a traditional "one-size-fits-all" approach to a culture that celebrates and implements personalized learning for every student?

2. What strategies can be employed to develop an educational environment where failure is seen as a learning opportunity, encouraging students and educators to embrace risk-taking?

3. Reflect on an "aha moment" you have experienced in your educational practice. How did this insight shape your approach to teaching and learning and how might it spur additional growth?

4. Considering the chapter's emphasis on the importance of culture for the success of personalized learning, what steps can be taken to develop or enhance elements within your educational setting?

5. What are some potential barriers to implementing the bold moves discussed in the chapter, and how might you address these challenges?

Share your progress on social media (Instagram, Twitter, LinkedIn, Facebook, TikTok) using the **#personalize** hashtag.

CHAPTER 2

Unveiling of Personalization

Imagine Maya, a budding artist who dreams of animating fantastical creatures. Traditional classrooms feel stifling–rows of desks, rote memorization, and tests that don't capture her vibrant imagination. Maya thrives on creativity, visual storytelling, and hands-on projects. Yet, the current system offers little room for her unique spark to ignite.

Personalized learning changes everything. It's transitioning from a rigid model to a dynamic landscape where Maya's artistic spirit can flourish. With personalized learning, Maya can tinker with animation software, explore digital art techniques, and collaborate with classmates on a stop-motion film project. Her learning becomes a pilgrimage of exploration, fueled by her passions and tailored to her needs. This is the power of personalized learning: igniting the unique potential within every student.

Establishing the Why

Education stands at a pivotal juncture. Emerging technologies have wrought profound transformations in the global landscape of work and life, a shift that has yielded positive outcomes in many instances but not without challenges. The undeniable truth is that change is not a distant prospect; it knocks daily at our doors. The conventional adage "that is how it has always been done" is steadily waning. As our times evolve, educational institutions worldwide are wrestling with the imperative of realigning their priorities to meet the ever-changing demands of society, an evolving workforce, novel fields of study, disruptive technologies, and students yearning for more relevant and individualized learning experiences. Consequently, numerous educational establishments are transitioning towards a more customized approach to education. It is time to innovate with purpose.

What makes something innovative? There is plenty of debate on this topic. That subject has been covered extensively, from articles to blog posts to books. One can look at numerous companies and develop their conclusions. Take Uber and Airbnb, for example. In their own right, each came up with a new and different idea aligned with technology to create something consumers would embrace while making money. Not only did both of these companies disrupt their respective industries, but both have evidence in the form of users and revenue to validate that their solutions were genuinely innovative. The convergence of an idea, tool, and strategy has led to the ultimate success of both Uber and Airbnb. Education can leverage these lessons to create new and better student learning experiences.

In education, it is tempting to jump on board the latest tool or idea and automatically stamp the word "innovation" on it. This is not to say that everything in these categories represents a better means to accomplish a task or improve professional practice. Not all innovations are suitable for education when repeatedly packed on top of each other, and we cannot assume that positive changes will always result. It is also important to note that "saying" something is innovative and actually "showing" that it is are two different things. The key is the criteria used to make such a determination or claim. In an educational context, innovation is creating, implementing, and sustaining ideas that improve learning based on evidence of impact. Whether to innovate or not should be driven by a challenge or problem that can be overcome in a way that leads to a better outcome. Achievement can undoubtedly fall into one of these categories, but there is so much more to learning and kids than a test score.

Personalized learning is a teaching approach that combines tailored instruction and pedagogy to equitably address each student's unique opportunities for growth, strengths, abilities, and interests. Personalized learning has the potential to revolutionize the educational landscape, increase student engagement and achievement, and better prepare learners for the challenges of a rapidly changing world (Chen & Wang, 2020; Shemshack & Spector, 2021; Tetzlaff et al., 2020). By customizing instruction to meet unique learner characteristics, educators can ensure that students receive the necessary support to overcome challenges. This approach can help bridge achievement gaps, allowing students to progress at their own pace, ensuring that they neither fall behind nor feel held back.

Furthermore, personalized learning promotes student engagement. When learners are actively involved in decisions about their education, they tend to be more motivated and interested in their studies. They can explore topics they are passionate about, which can lead to deeper understanding and a love for learning. This engagement is critical in an era where attention spans are shrinking, and distractions are abundant.

Personalization equips students with critical competencies for the future. In today's fast-paced, information-driven world, taking charge of learning, setting goals, and adapting to new challenges is invaluable. Personalized learning develops these competencies, preparing students to be independent, lifelong learners. They master content and how to learn, a skill that will serve them well throughout their lives.

Moreover, educators themselves benefit from personalized learning. It encourages teachers to be creative, flexible, and responsive to students. It enables them to better understand each student's abilities and challenges, which can lead to more effective teaching. Personalized learning can also reduce teacher burnout, providing a more rewarding and meaningful teaching experience. It represents a pivotal educational shift that caters to each student's individuality. By acknowledging the uniqueness of learners, promoting engagement, and preparing students for a rapidly changing world, personalized learning can help create a more effective and equitable education system. It is a path forward that benefits both students and educators, paving the way for a brighter, more adaptable future in education.

Defining Personalization

We define personalized learning as: all learners getting what they need, when and where they need it, to become life-ready. One thing is for sure: learning is not linear. Rarely does a student go from point A to point B in a straight line when it comes to acquiring and then constructing new knowledge and application to demonstrate conceptual understanding unless they are forced to do so. Many learners begin to struggle and lose confidence when this is the case. While a one-size-fits-all approach either worked for us or we just managed to get by, our connected world has shined a light on changes that can be made to maximize students' time in class. Herein lies the power of personalization.

In education, the quality of a lesson can significantly shape a student's classroom experience. Crafting a lesson plan is a time-consuming endeavor. We can all recollect numerous evenings and weekends when we dedicated countless hours to creating activities to keep our students involved and aligned with the prescribed curriculum standards. The focus should be on the overall learning experience, yet it is essential to emphasize that the lesson itself is the cornerstone upon which this enriching experience is built.

So, where do you begin the journey to personalized learning? The key to strengthening learning and instruction consists of the right balance of two main components:

1. Instruction (what the teacher does)
2. Learning (what the student does)

In the introduction, we presented the concept of shifting our focus from "what" to "who" to set the stage for personalization. The premise is as simple as it is powerful: to provide all learners with what they need, when and where they need it, to become life-ready. This approach underlines the importance of personalized learning environments

> The premise is as simple as it is powerful: to provide all learners with what they need, when and where they need it, to become life-ready.

that adapt and recognize that each learner's trajectory is unique and requires different supports at different times. While focusing on and knowing pertinent strategies is a good start, changing practice is what changes results. It is not enough to understand the benefits of personalized learning; educators must also actively work to implement these strategies within their classrooms and the curriculum.

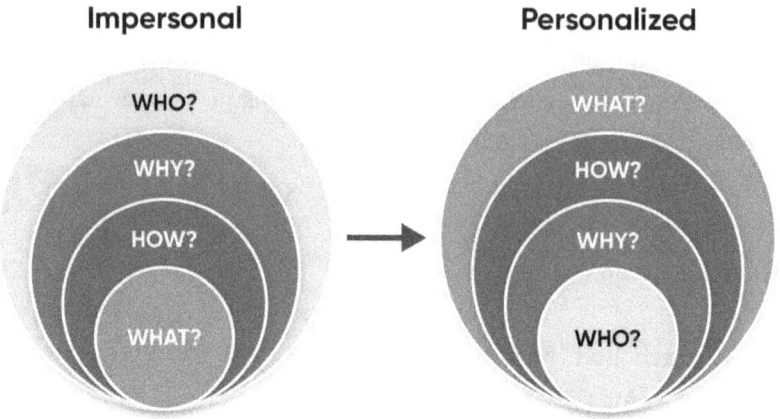

Striking a balance between teacher and student-centered instruction is of utmost importance. While there is a place for direct instruction, many learners strongly prefer other aspects of a lesson, ones they find more engaging and meaningful. Research supports that students desire a personalized learning experience, while educators seek alignment with global educational standards (Sheninger & Murray, 2017). Achieving common ground in this domain can often be a formidable task, but our kids and their future are worth the effort.

Making Instruction More Personal

Learning is a profound personal pursuit. Personalized learning increases engagement and helps learners better understand the subject matter. It all begins with understanding the learner's interests. What are they passionate about? What do they want to learn more about? Once you know the learner's interests, you can tailor the learning experience to them.

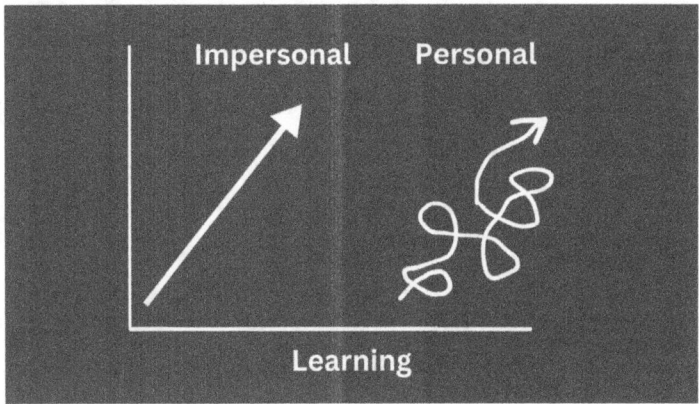

Here are things to consider, which can help make learning personal and empower students to take ownership of their education.

Establish Clarity

To make learning personal, educators should establish clear learning targets that are challenging and achievable for students. These should align with the standard(s) being addressed and the student's current knowledge and skills, ensuring they feel the appropriate cognitive flexibility without becoming overwhelmed. Clarity provides a sense of purpose, direction, and motivation, allowing students to measure their progress and take pride in their accomplishments. When facilitating Tier 1 instruction, look to impart relevance during the opening minutes through a well-designed anticipatory set or hook. At the conclusion, have the students reflect on how they will use what they learned outside the classroom as part of a closure task.

Determine Individual Needs

Data is the best tool educators can use to drive change, which will be discussed in detail in Chapter 5. There are many data sources, such as common formative assessments, routine benchmarks, and adaptive tools. You can even leverage data from exit tickets. By identifying both areas for growth and strengths, educators can begin to map out specific personalized pedagogical pathways that focus on customized supports. They can also adapt their teaching methods and materials.

Emphasize Choice and Autonomy

Empowering students with choice and autonomy is a fundamental aspect of personalized learning. When students can choose topics, tasks, projects, or how to demonstrate understanding, they become more invested in their learning. Educators can provide a range of options within the curriculum, allowing students to pursue their passions and explore their strengths while meeting educational objectives through choice activities, playlists, specific digital tools, dry-erase surfaces, and must-do/may-do options. This stimulates a sense of ownership and responsibility for their learning. Chapter 3 will cover this in more detail.

Provide Continuous Feedback and Support

Learning that is personal ensures continuous feedback to and support for students. Constructive feedback helps learners understand their strengths and areas for improvement, allowing them to adjust their strategies and take initiative in their learning journey. It should be timely, specific, and practical, with educators maintaining open lines of communication while offering customized guidance and resources. Also, embracing a growth mindset, where students understand that learning involves setbacks and challenges, can help them persevere and succeed.

Adapt and Evolve

Making learning personal is an ongoing process that requires adaptability, evolution, and growth. As students grow and change, so should their educational experiences. Educators should be willing to adapt their teaching methods and materials based on feedback and assessment results while connecting relevant trends and issues. Technology can also significantly create a personal touch, offering adaptive learning platforms and tools.

Relevant Thinking Framework

While incorporating these moves might seem daunting, there is a framework available that any educator can use to create a shared vision, language, and expectations when setting the stage for personalization. The Relevant Thinking Framework is an excellent tool for developing and analyzing questions, tasks, and assessments to ensure an appropriate amount of challenge and purposeful learning application.

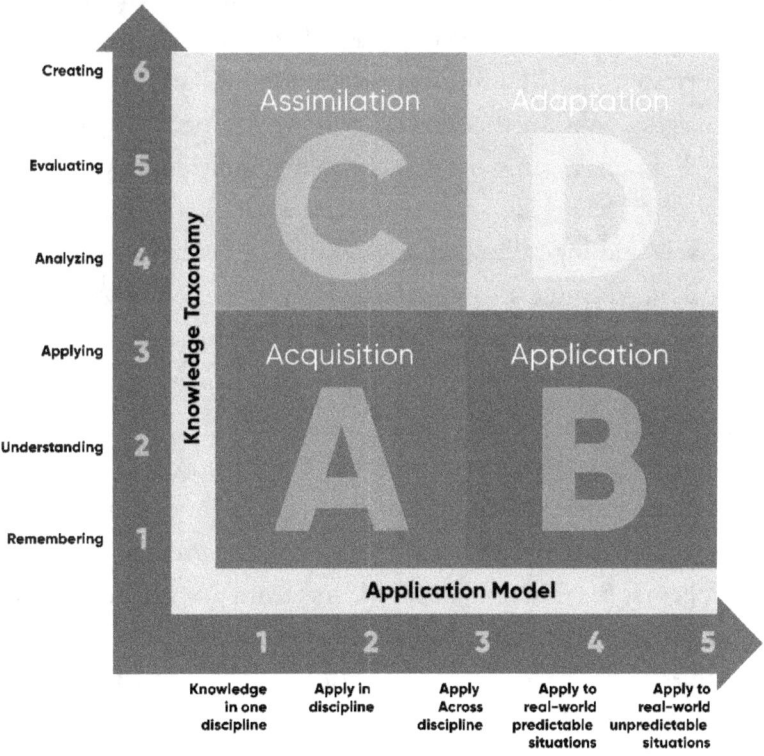

(Image adapted from the Center for Model Schools)

This model is an analytical instrument for evaluating curriculum and pedagogy, focusing on elevating standards and ensuring student success. It applies to crafting both teaching methods and evaluative measures. Furthermore, educators can employ this structure to track their advancement in integrating depth and applicability and determine fitting approaches for customizing instruction and achieving educational objectives.

The Knowledge Taxonomy (represented on the y-axis) spans a spectrum defined by the six tiers of Bloom's Taxonomy, which detail progressively intricate forms of cognition. Initially, the focus is on the assimilation of information and the capacity to retrieve or pinpoint that information. Analogous to how a computer searches for a word in a text editor, an individual adept at this stage can sift through an extensive array of data within the mind to find the needed information.

The upper tier of the Knowledge Taxonomy identifies increasingly intricate cognitive processes involved in utilizing and generating novel insights. Within this domain, knowledge becomes thoroughly ingrained in one's consciousness, enabling individuals to do more than retrieve facts—they can synthesize various information pieces innovatively and logically. This advanced stage could be aptly termed assimilation, reflecting a sophisticated level in the cognitive spectrum. It encompasses higher-order thinking skills where learners can address complex, multi-layered issues, crafting original creations, and formulating strategies.

The second spectrum (represented on the x-axis) is termed the Application Model. This model delineates a range of practical applications, encompassing five levels that define the execution of knowledge. Whereas the initial point of this spectrum pertains to knowledge gained for its intrinsic value, the apex represents application: employing the acquired knowledge to tackle intricate real-world challenges and to produce tangible projects, designs, and works intended for real-life application.

Below are descriptions of each quadrant:

A (Acquisition) — Learners accumulate and store diverse information and insights. The primary expectation is that students recall or comprehend this information. For instance, understanding that the moon is spherical is an example of knowledge in Quadrant A.

B (Application) — Students utilize their gathered knowledge to address problems, devise solutions, and execute tasks. The pinnacle of this stage is applying knowledge to novel and unforeseen circumstances. An illustrative example is using mathematical understanding to manage financial transactions and calculate change.

C (Assimilation) — Students enhance and refine their existing knowledge to the point where it can be applied spontaneously and habitually in problem analysis and solution development. At this stage, learners engage with more advanced knowledge, such as comprehending the intricacies of a nation's political system and examining the merits and challenges posed by that nation's cultural diversity compared to others.

D (Adaptation) — Learners are adept at intricate thought processes. One example is the capacity to navigate wide-area network systems to acquire information and utilize various sources to tackle a complex issue professionally.

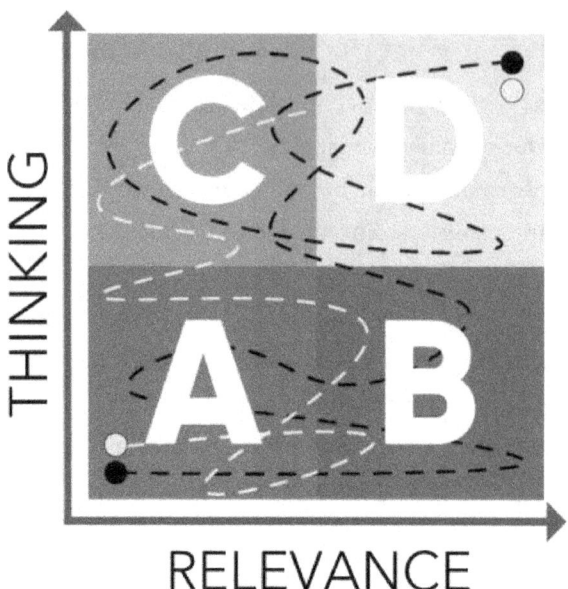

RELEVANCE

The journey to quad D is always dynamic. It will also look different for every learner, so do not stay focused on where the dots are on the image above. Authenticity, more profound meaning, academy programs, and other ways to show learning are just as powerful in providing kids with what they need to succeed. As students work to answer scaffolded questions while grappling with solving real-world problems, their process will look different. Hence, there will be many learning paths towards and eventually into Quad D.

The best classroom management strategy is sound pedagogy. Making learning personal can help establish attentive behavior while creating an environment where students *want* to work. Some practical tips can be leveraged during every lesson:

> The best classroom management strategy is sound pedagogy.

✦ Integrate a hook at the beginning of class.

✦ Use technology to create interactive and engaging learning experiences.

✦ Connect learning to the learner's real-world experiences.

✦ Encourage learners to reflect on their learning and set goals for themselves.

✦ Celebrate the learner's successes.

Personalized learning is a powerful educational approach that recognizes each student's uniqueness. Educators can create an environment where students are actively engaged and take ownership of their learning by assessing learning preferences, establishing clarity, offering choice and autonomy, providing continuous feedback and support, and adapting to changing needs. Personalization enhances academic achievement and instills a love for learning that extends beyond the classroom.

The Role of Technology

While there are many ways to personalize without technology, tools now provide endless opportunities to address gaps and offer more challenges. Education and the digital realm are now fundamentally interlinked. Both learners and educators are deeply embedded in digital experiences and require more efficient, targeted strategies for leveraging digital tools in meaningful and academically rigorous ways to bolster learning. Research has shown that technology can have a positive impact on achievement, motivation, and engagement (Alsuwaiyan & Alharbi, 2021; AlQahtani & Alharbi, 2021; Chen & Zang, 2021; Lai & Yuen, 2021; Lee & Choi, 2022; Murillo-Zamorano et al., 2020). The key is practical design. Educators need to craft and implement instructional approaches that are both relevant and challenging, while incorporating practical digital resources to reinforce their teaching.

Provided educators focus on educational goals, digital tools can serve as a potent resource to enhance instruction and learning.

While there are many different frameworks regarding effective technology integration, SAMR is typically the one that most people and schools leverage. At face value, it is straightforward while conveying how technology can move from enhancement to transformation. The SAMR Model (Puentedura, 2010) has provided us with an excellent lens to observe firsthand the need for proper planning before investing large amounts of money in technology. This is not a perfect framework to guide the effective implementation of technology initiatives, but it gives us a good idea of what should not occur.

Substitution – tech acts as a direct tool substitute with no functional change

Augmentation – tech acts as a direct tool substitute with functional improvement

Modification – tech allows for significant task redesign

Redefinition – tech allows for the creation of new tasks previously inconceivable

While we do not outright discount SAMR, it does have a dramatic shortcoming. SAMR is a catchy model with some value, mainly in what we should not do (substitution). Take a close look at the tech-centric language used in each category and ask what the SAMR model depicts about the level of student learning (Sheninger, 2015). This is why we love the Relevant Thinking Framework to ensure that technology is integrated effectively. It provides a common language, constitutes the lens through which to examine all aspects of learning (curriculum, instruction, assessment), and helps create a culture around a shared vision.

The value of SAMR is that it can inform educators what NOT to do with technology. However, the rub is that it needs to be more specific regarding the pedagogical shifts needed to improve student learning. Here is where the Relevant Thinking Framework comes into play, as there is an emphasis on what the learner is doing instead of the technology. While there is not a seamless alignment, here is how they can connect to help empower learners through the purposeful use of technology to personalize:

(S) Substituted acquisition (A) Teachers use tech to make tasks digital or elicit low-level student responses

(A) Applied augmentation (B) Students apply learning in relevant ways

(M) Modified assimilation (C) Students demonstrate high levels of thinking through the purposeful use of technology

(R) Adapted redefinition (D) – Students work and think to innovatively redefine what is possible

Relevant Thinking Framework

(emphasis on what learner is doing)

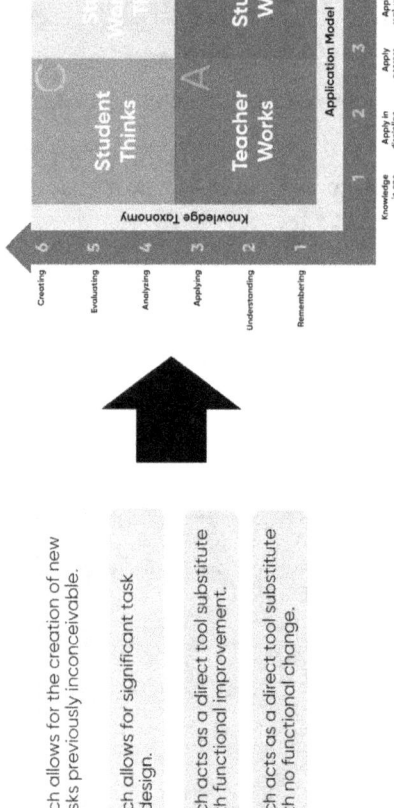

SAMR Model

(emphasis on what **not** to do with tech)

Redefinition
- tech allows for the creation of new tasks previously inconceivable.

Modification
- tech allows for significant task redesign.

Augmentation
- tech acts as a direct tool substitute with functional improvement.

Substitution
- tech acts as a direct tool substitute with no functional change.

The overall goal, both with and without technology, should be to empower students to work and think. Another critical strategy is to focus on the purposeful use of technology when appropriate. Just because it is available does not mean it can or will improve every lesson or project. Thus, if appropriate, focusing on pedagogy first and then technology second will help ensure success. While SAMR is a solid starting point, it is not the end-all or be-all. The multi-dimensional aspects of the Relevant Thinking Framework can be used to guide the development of better questions and tasks as part of good pedagogy. Appendix 1 provides a comprehensive list of technology tools that teachers can leverage, including artificial intelligence (AI).

It is important to note that Bloom's Taxonomy and SAMR are not new approaches. However, there is an opportunity to grow regarding relevance, level of thinking, and the purposeful use of technology. These elements are essential when it comes to personalization. One of the greatest assets you possess is the ability to self-reflect in these areas to set the stage to unlock the potential of your students.

Personalized Approach

Moving forward with the changes discussed in this chapter requires a refined vision and leadership at all levels. The pursuit towards a personalized learning culture in schools begins with a detailed assessment of the current educational landscape. This crucial first step involves gathering insights into existing instructional methods, curriculum alignment, and student engagement mechanisms. Educators and administrators must dive deep into understanding their student population. This can be achieved through comprehensive surveys, interviews with students, teachers, and parents, as well as classroom observations. The goal is to pinpoint the gaps between current classroom or school learning practices and the personalized approach desired. By identifying these discrepancies, schools can outline a clear, actionable roadmap tailored to bridge these gaps, ensuring that the move towards personalization is strategic and grounded in shared goals.

Following the assessment phase, the focus shifts towards curriculum and instructional design, recognizing these as foundational pillars in personalized learning architecture. The curriculum must be re-envisioned not as a static entity, but as a dynamic framework that offers flexibility, choice, and adaptability to cater to individual learning trajectories. This involves integrating project-based learning, competency-based assessments, and adaptive learning technologies that adjust to learners' pace and preferences. Teachers are pivotal in this transformation, acting as facilitators who guide, mentor, and adjust learning paths based on real-time data and student feedback. Professional learning becomes paramount in this context, equipping educators with the necessary skills and understanding to navigate and thrive in a personalized learning environment. Training sessions, workshops, and collaborative planning time allow teachers to explore innovative pedagogies, technology integration, and differentiated instruction techniques essential for personalization.

Finally, implementing a personalized learning approach hinges on the effective use of technology. Digital infrastructure must be in place to support individualized learning experiences, including learning management systems that offer personalized content and data analytics tools that provide insights into student progress and areas for improvement. However, more than technology is needed; moving to personalization requires the entire school community's active involvement and support. This means engaging students, parents, and teachers in meaningful conversations about the value and implementation of personalized learning, ensuring their understanding and support. Continuous feedback mechanisms and a commitment to adjusting approaches based on what works well are essential. By weaving together the threads of community engagement, curriculum flexibility, and professional development, schools can transform their learning environments into spaces where every student feels valued, understood, and empowered to reach their full potential.

The transformation towards a personalized learning implementation is not just an educational move but a bold leap into innovation and risk-taking. Embracing this journey requires schools to step out of their comfort zones and challenge traditional teaching and learning paradigms. It is a move that necessitates a mindset where risk-taking is celebrated, not shunned, understanding that the path to personalization is paved with trials, errors, and profound learning experiences. By encouraging educators and students to experiment with new pedagogies, technologies, and learning formats, schools can usher in an environment that is not only conducive to personalized learning but also vibrant with innovation. Innovation acts as the lifeblood of personalized education, ensuring that the learning experiences continuously evolve, reflecting the latest educational research, technological advancements, and the learning gaps of the student body. In this dynamic setting, personalized learning transitions from concept to reality, offering tailored educational experiences that resonate with and engage every student.

Professional learning emerges as a cornerstone in building this innovative and risk-taking culture, equipping educators with the new skills and mindsets required for personalization. Continuous professional development opportunities that focus on the principles of personalized learning, such as student agency, data-informed instruction, and technology integration, are vital. Workshops, seminars, and collaborative learning sessions become arenas for educators to share insights, challenges, and successes related to practice that is deeply invested in reimagining education. This professional learning is not a one-time event but a career-long expedition, where educators are seen as learners, always seeking to refine their craft and adapt to the changing educational landscape. Through this lens, professional development supports not just the acquisition of new teaching strategies but the cultivation of a growth mindset among educators—a mindset essential for the iterative, experimental nature of personalized learning.

Feedback is the final, critical piece of the puzzle, ensuring that the journey toward personalized learning is informed and reflective. In a culture that values innovation and risk-taking, feedback acts as a compass, guiding adjustments and nurturing ongoing improvement. This feedback should be multi-directional, involving not just educator-to-educator or student-to-educator exchanges but also encompassing the wider school community's perspectives, including parents and external partners. Embracing feedback requires trust and openness, where all voices are heard and valued. This openness to feedback allows schools to fine-tune their approaches to personalized learning, ensuring that innovation is always grounded in students' real-world experiences and outcomes. Together, risk-taking, embracing innovation, professional learning, and openness to feedback create a powerful synergy, driving the evolution of schools toward vibrant, personalized learning where every student's potential can be fully realized.

Bold Moves

Educators can revolutionize learning by weaving personalization into their classrooms. This means customizing lessons to each student's strengths, interests, and what makes their learning stick. It is a shift from the traditional, cookie-cutter approach to a flexible, student-centered one. By harnessing technology and innovative teaching methods, educators can craft dynamic environments where students go deep into the material and own their educational trajectories.

But to make personalized learning truly sing, it requires a system-wide makeover of culture, including curriculum design, how we assess learning, and how teachers are prepared. Schools should transform into places where students feel celebrated and supported on their unique learning paths, instilling a sense of ownership and responsibility for their education. This cultural move supercharges student engagement and motivation. It equips them for our world's complexities, ensuring they graduate with the critical thinking, problem-solving, and lifelong learning skills they'll need to thrive.

Bold moves demand brave steps. This occurs when we contemplate our methods and identify a better approach to develop in ways that defy traditional beliefs or our initial training. The following questions are designed to guide you on this path.

1. How am I personalizing learning to meet the unique needs of each student in my classroom? If not, what initial steps need to be taken?

2. How is technology being leveraged in a purposeful way to enhance personalized learning experiences?

3. What strategies am I using to encourage student ownership in their learning process? How can the Relevant Thinking Framework help?

4. How do I measure the effectiveness of personalized learning strategies in improving student engagement and achievement?

5. What professional development opportunities can I pursue to better support personalized learning in my classroom or school?

Share your progress on social media (Instagram, Twitter, LinkedIn, Facebook, TikTok) using the **#personalize** hashtag.

CHAPTER 3

Empowering Students Through Agency

At Westview High, Jamie found herself lost in the crowd. Despite being a sophomore, she had yet to find her place or passion within the walls of her high school. That was until a new personalized learning program was introduced to increase student agency. Assigned to a project that required students to explore and address a real-world problem, Jamie discovered her interest in mental health awareness. With the freedom to choose her project's direction, she decided to create a digital platform that provided resources and support for teenagers struggling with anxiety and depression.

Under the mentorship of Ms. Thompson, an advocate for personalized learning, Jamie embarked on an adventure of self-discovery and empowerment. She researched, designed, and launched her website, learning coding, digital design, and effective communication. The project allowed Jamie to pursue a subject she was passionate about and equipped her with skills and confidence she never knew she possessed.

As her project gained recognition within the school and the wider community, Jamie transformed from a quiet student into a leader and advocate for mental health. The personalized learning program at Westview High allowed her to explore her interests deeply, leading to a profound personal and academic transformation.

The story above illustrates the importance of student agency. It is pivotal in classrooms as it increases active engagement, ownership of learning, and the development of crucial competencies. When students are encouraged to have a say in their educational journey, they become more invested in learning. This heightened engagement makes the classroom experience more enjoyable and improves academic outcomes. Students who are active participants in their learning tend to develop a deeper understanding of the subject matter and are more motivated to explore topics beyond the curriculum. Research highlights the importance of student agency for supporting engagement, learning, and empowerment as it builds the capacity to act independently and make choices, which is crucial for the learning process (Vaughn, 2021).

There are many ways to engage and empower students that lead to ownership of learning, creating what we call a "free-range" experience that replicates real-world contexts and develops critical competencies while tapping into passions. While there are many strategies a teacher can use to accomplish this, focusing on high-agency elements is powerful and realistic. These elements include voice, choice, path, pace, and place.

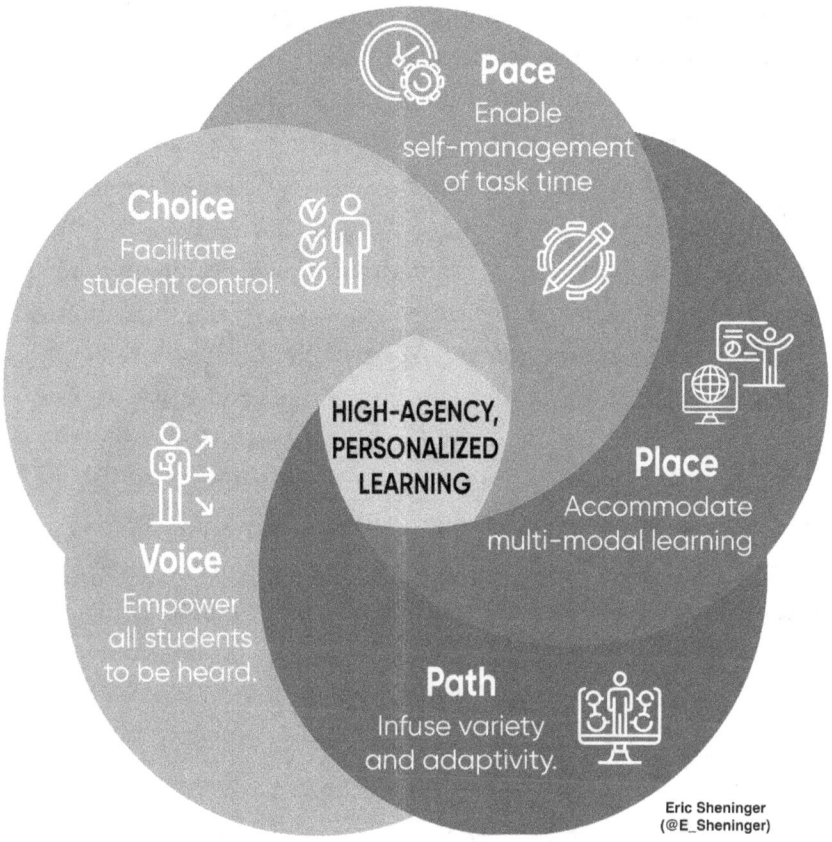

Eric Sheninger
(@E_Sheninger)

Amplifying Voice

Honoring students' voices and allowing them to have a say during the learning process is a central tenet of student agency. Acknowledging children's perspectives and affording them an active role in their education stands as a foundational principle of student voice. Various interpretations of this principle exist, with some being expansive enough to encompass how students can be granted the authority to utilize their voices to enhance the learning environment. It includes the authentic input of students or their leadership within the realms of instruction, school infrastructure, or educational policies, all of which have the potential to instigate substantial alterations within educational systems, practices, and policies by endowing students with the capacity to be catalysts for change, frequently collaborating with adult educators.

In the classroom, student voice can occur by presenting questions or challenges for students to tackle, enabling them to use digital tools for responses encompassing text, video, audio, drawings, imagery, and gifs. A non-digital illustration involves students presenting their thoughts on a whiteboard for the teacher's review. Often, anonymity amplifies voices, serving as a crucial asset for introverted and reserved students. Furthermore, they can be offered opportunities to contribute viewpoints regarding classroom arrangements, evaluations, and feedback. Student voice denotes any action that empowers students to express their perspectives when shaping their learning journey. The primary message here is that classroom participation is all-inclusive, promoting a greater sense of involvement for everyone.

Student voice.....

- Involves all kids in the learning process.
- Fosters active participation.
- Builds confidence leading to self-efficacy, especially when students can respond under cover of anonymity.
- Promotes open reflection and collaboration.
- Sets the stage for instant feedback.
- Develops a sense of community.

It is crucial to understand that there is no one right way to amplify student voice. It could be as simple as all kids using an individual whiteboard or dry-erase surface to respond. Technology also provides an ever-growing selection of tools that involve kids in the learning process in ways that lead to greater empowerment. Think about how audio, video, or the ability to draw can help a child find their voice. At a macro level, open forums and surveys can elicit ideas for improvement. The point is that voice takes on many forms, each with positive outcomes.

Teachers in the Corinth School District in Corinth, MS, embraced student voice. For the most part, technology has been their pathway of choice, where tools such as Blooket, Gimkit, Mentimeter, Padlet, Edpuzzle, Nearpod, and Kahoot have been integrated into instruction. Many of the strategies are simple yet highly effective. Look at this short video clip of a textbook-personalized classroom using sound blended pedagogies. It can be accessed at bit.ly/PLcorinthA or using the QR code. The opening frame shows a choice board that students could access in Canvas, along with standards-aligned learning targets. As the video progresses, see if you can identify the voice strategy this teacher developed.

Were you able to identify the strategy? At first, it might have been hard to catch it because you were probably impressed with the choice board and observable evidence of how empowered the learners were. Looking closely, you will see that some computers had a green clothespin attached to the top while the group at the end of the clip had a red one.

When a question or challenge arose, the students would clip the red one to their laptops. This signified to the teacher that a group needed help. At the end of the video, you see where some students were getting needed support. If everything was good, the green clip remained on the computer. Not only was this an effective way to include student voice, but it also allowed the teacher to focus her time on the learners who needed it the most.

We see student voice as the gateway to personalization. Educators can quickly implement it as part of Tier 1 instruction, allowing students to report during cooperative learning, projects, and choice activities. It can also enable students to advocate for needed changes to school culture. You would be hard-pressed to find a more valuable strategy that is universal across virtually all pedagogical techniques. The reason for this statement is straightforward. For learning to occur, students both need and want to be involved. If the goal is to engage kids and set the stage for empowerment, it is critical to utilize strategies that amplify student voices.

As you look to include or improve student voice in your classroom (or school), keep in mind the intended outcomes. Work backward from there and find the strategy that works best for your learners, and feel free to mix it up now and again. Ultimately, it is difficult for kids to own their learning if they do not have a say.

Ownership through Choice

Agency in the classroom is about giving students more control over their learning through greater autonomy and purpose. It is driven by many factors, one of which is choice. The underlying premise is to move learners from a state of engagement to empowerment so that they exert more ownership over their learning. One of the simplest ways of employee empowerment is to give them the choice to approach their work. The underlying idea in this approach is that choice gives employees a sense of personal control, which can enhance their intrinsic motivation towards their work, resulting in higher morale, creativity, innovation, better performance, more significant organizational commitment, and lower turnover (Chua & Iyengar, 2006). Much like employees in the workplace, students in classrooms are empowered by clear expectations, supportive feedback, and opportunities to make choices that affect their learning experiences.

Understanding just how critical choice can be when thinking about lesson design and pedagogy is essential. Just like any strategy, there is not one best way to integrate choice. Implementing it in the classroom can be as simple as allowing students to choose how to demonstrate understanding, a certain number of activities to complete, or selecting the right tool for a specified task. The bottom line is not to overthink choice when getting started with this high-agency strategy.

We consistently see several strategies integrated with a high degree of fidelity worldwide. These include must-do/may-do activities, choice boards, and playlists. Each gives students greater control over their learning while freeing up the teacher for targeted instruction or support. Best of all, there are unlimited possibilities for creating these activities.

Must-do / May-do

As presenters and coaches, we show the value of various strategies educators can implement. We always point out that what might work for one person or classroom might not necessarily be the best fit for others. Do not think you need to create an elaborate board. A must-do/may-do menu is a great option that we see used effectively:

MUST-DO	MAY-DO
Purposeful and well-designed tasks aligned to standards that allow students to practice, develop understanding, think critically, and apply their learning.	Relevant and engaging extension activities that cater to interests, learning paths, and deeper exploration of concepts.

Eric Sheninger (@E_Sheninger)

Before implementing this personalized strategy, determine how the tasks will align with the standard(s) that are the focal point of the mini-lesson it will follow. Remember the inherent value of tried-and-true instructional strategies where personalization can be integrated through student voice, such as reviews of prior learning, checks for understanding, and closure. The next step is to develop substantive tasks that all students must complete and choices they may engage in afterward.

In the real world, individuals often have choices in approaching tasks and projects. Must-do/may-do activities mirror this reality and prepare students for decision-making and time-management skills they will need later in life. Their value extends even further. In every classroom, students have different strengths and weaknesses. Must-do/may-do activities allow students to choose tasks that align with their abilities. This flexibility can reduce frustration for struggling students and prevent boredom for advanced ones.

Must-do/may-do tasks support students at various competency levels, encourage autonomy, and prepare students for the complexities of the real world, all of which contribute to a more effective and enriching educational experience. Most of all, they can free up teacher time to support those learners who need it the most.

Choice Boards

Choice boards are a highly effective personalized learning strategy, offering opportunities to scaffold tasks, provide differentiation, and incorporate various digital and non-digital options. They play a significant role in classrooms because they enhance student engagement and provide autonomy. Choice boards empower students by allowing them to select from several learning activities while facilitating differentiation. Teachers can design choice boards with various activities catering to multiple readiness levels and learning preferences. This ensures that every student can access content at an appropriate level and in a manner that suits their learning preference and interests.

Getting these set up is pretty simple. Following a short mini-lesson, students are given an array of scaffolded options where they select only a certain number to complete. One of the most common options is modeled after Tic-Tac-Toe. While the class works, the teacher pulls students based on data for 1:1 support. Differentiation can occur by making available different versions based on ability derived from data. It is also important to note that the number of choices is up to the educator. Don't think there must be six or nine options because of how a template is structured.

Students can choose activities that align with their strengths and interests, allowing them to excel in areas they are passionate about while also challenging themselves to grow in other skill areas. This holistic approach to skill development prepares students for success in various academic and real-world situations. By making choices and reflecting on their outcomes, students become more adept at setting personal learning goals and monitoring their progress. This metacognitive skill is essential for lifelong learning and personal growth.

Playlists

Picture a school scenario where students begin their day by entering the classroom and using their devices to scan a distinct QR code or log into a learning management system and access a curated set of activities tailored to their specific learning requirements. Subsequently, when the teacher arrives in the classroom shortly after, they engage in brief one-on-one conferences with each student, discussing their progress while the remaining students diligently carry on with their assigned tasks. Playlists are a simple strategy that packs immense power.

A playlist in an educational context is essentially an assignment designed to enable students to engage in learning tasks at their preferred pace and in the order they choose. The transfer of responsibility for executing the learning plan sets playlists apart from traditional teaching methods. Here, students are provided with a list of tasks upfront, including access to supporting content and digital tools if required. While the scenario at the beginning of this section highlights how technology can be used, playlists can be just as effective on paper.

Armed with this comprehensive learning plan, students embark on their educational journey, working through the assignments at a pace that suits their unique learning preferences and capabilities. Furthermore, playlists often come in digital copies, conveniently delivered through platforms like Google Classroom, Schoology, or Canvas. This digital aspect allows teachers to personalize the playlists that target learner needs.

Playlists significantly depart from traditional teaching methods, promoting student autonomy, personalization, and adaptability. While most of the class progresses through the playlist, teachers can work one-on-one with students who need the most assistance. Herein lies one of the most essential elements of any personalized experience–kids getting help who need it the most.

One day, we received a text message from Nathan Hall, the principal of Corinth Middle School in Mississippi.. He shared an image during a walk-through of a choice activity that Betty Graham, one of his 8th-grade teachers, successfully implemented. She explained that during an intercession (an extended break based on the district's year-long calendar) some of her students asked if she could bring back the board they could click on because they enjoyed it so much. They said it was easier to follow. So, after spring break, she worked on making a board for her students. They wanted the links so they would not have to click different places. With this board, they knew what they must do daily and weekly and what to do when finished. One thing she liked about the board was that she did not hear, "What do I do now?" Students were now always working. When she asked one period what they liked about the board, they said it was easy to follow, plus they loved the links.

Watching Betty and her colleagues at Corinth Middle School grow with choice was incredible. Thinking about what she created, we cannot help but reflect on all the many different choice activities we have seen in classrooms or those shared virtually. Integrating challenging and relevant choices into the daily learning routine is one of the simplest yet most impactful elements, enhancing students' engagement and promoting a sense of agency in the classroom and beyond.

Here are some tips to consider as you develop, refine, or provide feedback on choice activities.

+ Develop a template and embed it in your learning management system (LMS) for easy access if digital tools are incorporated.
+ Ensure alignment to the mini-lesson (content and concept specific) or areas of need (intervention).
+ Provide clear expectations.
+ Shy away from all tech options.
+ Include a challenging and relevant task(s).
+ Try to avoid overloading with too many activities.
+ Integrate adaptive tools that respond to strengths and weaknesses while acquiring data that can be used for groupings and improving instruction.
+ Display a timer to aid in self-regulation and pacing.
+ Consider differentiating by having at least two variations.
+ Use data to pull individuals for 1:1 support when the entire class works.
+ Make time to monitor in between 1:1 support.
+ End the lesson with a closure task (i.e., exit ticket) for learner accountability and teacher feedback by creating a simple formative assessment for learners to complete when finished with all activities. This could consist simply of 3 scaffolded questions.

Not only does this provide closure, but it will also provide insight into whether the kids engaged in all the tasks.

Choice is the great differentiator that helps meet ALL learners' needs. It can be as simple as choosing the right tool for a task, a research paper topic, or how to create a product to demonstrate learning. The key is always looking for opportunities to include choice and voice during each lesson.

Different Ways to Show Learning

For many of us, our preparation to become teachers consisted of courses focusing on classroom management, lesson design, grading, and proven strategies that had withstood the test of time. We were also exposed to learning style theory and its many benefits. To this day, it is still heavily referenced, even though it has been largely debunked.

Popularity alone does not guarantee accuracy. A recent analysis of the scientific literature concerning learning styles reveals limited evidence that unequivocally supports the notion that matching instructional methods with an individual's learning style leads to better outcomes (Pashar et al., 2008). In contrast, several studies challenge this assumption (Massa & Mayer, 2008). It is evident that people often have well-defined learning preferences, such as visual, kinesthetic, or intuitive, but it remains uncertain whether these preferences significantly impact learning outcomes. The prevailing idea needs more substantial scientific backing, while more robust evidence supports alternative learning strategies.

Research continues to provide further evidence that the conventional wisdom about learning styles should be rejected by educators and students alike (Kirschner, 2017; Husmann & O'Loughlin, 2018; Riener & Willingham, 2010). While this challenge to conventional wisdom might be hard to swallow, some good news comes as a silver lining. There are better ways to learn, because the paths and preferences of people vary. Hence, there is a need to incorporate an array of strategies that pull on the strengths of some learners while addressing weaknesses in others.

We have outlined various personalized strategies that can be implemented after a mini-lesson is facilitated to incorporate voice and choice. While these take some planning upfront, some simpler techniques can be readily integrated into any lesson in the form of voice and choice. When reviewing prior learning, checking for understanding, or closing lessons, allow students to choose how to show what they have learned through the following means:

+ Writing (digital tools, individual whiteboards)
+ Video
+ Audio
+ Images
+ Drawing (digital tools and individual whiteboards)

To see an innovative example, check out this video at bit.ly/ PLcorinthB or using this QR code:

While technology presents a myriad of options for students to demonstrate learning, traditional mini whiteboards can also be used in some cases. None of the pathways above are meant to replace summative assessments. However, using varied formative means caters to a learner's preference by giving them the best opportunity to show what they have learned. It builds confidence, stimulates creativity, and empowers students during lessons.

We All Learn at a Different Pace

We must all acknowledge a fundamental truth: We each embark on the learning path at our own unique pace. This concept is deeply rooted in education and cognitive psychology, a realization that stems from experiences, knowledge, cognitive abilities, and learning preferences that define each of us. These factors profoundly influence the speed at which we absorb new knowledge and skills.

To truly understand our students, we must acknowledge their strengths and weaknesses while appreciating the role of their prior knowledge and experiences in shaping their learning trajectories. During the "get-to-know-you" phase, it is equally vital to identify how students learn best; as we all know, we do not all absorb information in the same way. Moreover, we harbor varying cognitive abilities—memory, attention, processing speed—and these faculties undoubtedly play a pivotal role in rapidly grasping new concepts and retaining information. It is abundantly clear that the one-size-fits-all approach is ill-suited to students of the present and future.

Introducing a self-paced learning approach, particularly for specific subjects, empowers our students to assume the driver's seat in their educational journey. It is a move that grants them the reins of control, allowing them to dictate the pace of their progress. However, this empowerment must be accompanied by the necessary support and resources, even if it means some students advance at a different rate in certain areas. We must constantly ask ourselves: Are we challenging each student at their ability level? Are we providing tailored pathways that align with each student's unique requirements? Are we giving our high achievers the space to soar? If the answer is "No," then we must reconsider our approaches.

Implementing self-paced learning opportunities is easier than it might initially seem. Think of it in terms of fitness programs. Nearly everyone has set a fitness goal at some point in their lives. In both fitness and self-paced learning, personal responsibility is inextricably linked to individual motivation, goal setting, tracking progress, and maintaining consistency. While external support and feedback hold value, the ultimate responsibility for progress and success rests with the individual.

Just as fitness enthusiasts set SMART goals, students establish learning objectives, whether it's mastering a new skill, passing an exam, or completing a grade-level course ahead of schedule. Achieving these goals becomes a measure of their accountability. Tracking progress is indispensable for ensuring those goals are met, just as we use measurements, scales, and fitness apps to monitor our physical progress. In a self-paced learning program, students employ tools like rubrics, feedback, journals, to-do lists, planners, and student trackers to monitor their academic growth.

Consistency is the linchpin. Regular workouts, a balanced diet, and adequate recovery are essential in fitness. Similarly, students must adhere to a consistent study schedule to make meaningful progress. Self-monitoring and self-reflection are equally vital. In fitness, we pay heed to our bodies, adjusting workouts and diets based on how we feel and perform. Likewise, in self-paced learning, individuals must gauge their level of understanding using rubrics and other tools and identify gaps in their education.

Feedback and communication from trainers or teachers are crucial for growth. They help individuals learn from their mistakes and receive guidance on staying on track with their goals. Intrinsic motivation, the grand motivator, replaces the "game of school" or the mimicry of diets. Empowering learners to take charge of their educational success, allowing them to reach their goals or maintain a healthy lifestyle, sets the benchmark for truly effective teaching.

The role of educators is to guide, mentor, coach, and facilitate learning, cultivating critical thinkers who are independent and confident in problem-solving. Conversely, the one-size-fits-all approach hinders this goal by treating students as if they were automatons rather than nurturing problem-solvers who can communicate effectively. Recognizing and respecting diversity in the pace of learning is a cornerstone of education. The ultimate objective is to provide each student with the unwavering support and resources required to realize their full potential, each on their unique journey.

> The ultimate objective is to provide each student with the unwavering support and resources required to realize their full potential, each on their unique journey.

Self-Paced Learning in Action

At Quest Academy Jr. High in West Haven, UT, the foremost aspiration of educators is clear: to mold their students into independent, lifelong learners. To bring this vision to life, Quest devised an innovative self-paced math program, a powerful vehicle that places students squarely in the driver's seat of their educational odyssey.

Quest's math program is set apart by using a dynamic video-based curriculum resembling the innovative flipped classroom approach. This instructional engine is further augmented by a digital practice platform known as Edgenuity, which works in tandem to deliver the initial lessons. At Quest, each teacher painstakingly forges a personalized course for every student, meticulously charting a pathway aligned with state core standards. Educators hold the power to tailor a course for their students, adjusting the content as needed to bridge any gaps in comprehension. The students, in turn, embark on their learning pursuit at their own pace, only advancing to the next lesson or standard once they have demonstrated mastery.

However, Quest's self-paced program is not just about customization, but also a finely tuned assessment tool. The video curriculum serves as the conduit for the initial instruction and provides real-time formative assessment data. Armed with this insight, teachers engage students in small group or one-on-one interactions, where they can provide individualized support and practice as necessary.

Each course is neatly compartmentalized into approximately twelve standards within this pedagogical framework. Upon completion of each standard, students close their laptops and pick up pen and paper for a tangible assessment called "Prove-its." These assessments are the litmus test for comprehension, a barometer of their knowledge retention. If a student proves ready, they proceed to take the "Prove-It" and advance to the next standard. For those who are not quite ready, teachers lead them in small group sessions to work on the challenging concepts and provide additional practice until they are primed to tackle a fresh "Prove-It." Quest's exacting standards demand that students cannot move forward until they can indeed prove their understanding.

The story above represents a Secondary Math 1 class featuring 7th, 8th, and 9th graders, all laboring harmoniously together. Thanks to this accessible program, Quest's students can traverse their academic terrain whenever and wherever they choose. Every year, some students surge ahead of the curve, often completing two grade levels of math in a single academic year. Nevertheless, in the crucible of Quest's "Prove-its," the institution ensured that students had truly mastered the content, preparing them for the impending end-of-level assessments.

For those who completed their current grade level standards, a significant opportunity beckoned: the chance to ascend to the next grade level. Ambitious students who outpaced their peers had the luxury of advancing at their own velocity each year. This remarkable flexibility allowed some to conclude high school math courses by the end of their 9th-grade year, earning an extra high school credit toward graduation.

Quest's philosophy of empowering students to steer their own inquiry kindled a fiery passion for learning and instilled a profound appreciation for the educational process. The Quest Academy's self-paced math program was more than a pedagogical tool; it was a transformative force, nurturing independent thinkers and lifelong learners.

All Paths are Unique

Learning is a unique and intricate process, with each learner embarking on their own distinctive path towards success. The idea that every individual follows a different route to achieve their goals is deeply rooted in the nature of human cognition, aspirations, and experiences. Let us explore the fundamental reasons why every learner carries out a distinct educational journey, acknowledging the multifaceted elements contributing to this diversity.

Cognitive science has demonstrated that no two minds are alike, and individuals possess distinct learning preferences, strengths, and weaknesses (Wen et al., 2022). Some learners may excel in visual or kinesthetic learning, while others lean towards auditory or logical approaches. These intrinsic differences in how we process information and tackle challenges lead to the development of personalized learning pathways, as individuals naturally gravitate towards methods that resonate with their cognitive preferences.

Furthermore, learners' varying motivations, interests, and aspirations play a pivotal role in shaping how they learn. While one student might be passionately driven by a desire to explore the realms of science and engineering, another may find their calling in the world of art and literature. These unique interests and objectives guide individuals toward specific areas of study and influence the choices they make in their learning endeavors. Learners' distinct paths reflect their personal quests to align their educational experiences with their passions and long-term aspirations.

A learning path is a high-agency strategy for personalization. It is a dynamic and flexible framework that empowers learners to take control of their educational journey. Here are some essential outcomes associated with strategies that allow students to follow their own path:

+ **Customized Content Selection:** Students have the autonomy to select the content, resources, and materials that resonate with their interests and learning preferences. This approach acknowledges that learners are more engaged and motivated when they have a say in what they study.

+ **Setting Individual Goals and Progression:** Students are encouraged to develop their own learning objectives and goals. They have the flexibility to spend more time on challenging topics and accelerate through areas where they excel, ensuring a comfortable and effective learning experience.

+ **Learning Needs and Preferences:** These acknowledge the diversity of how learners' progress and succeed. Students can choose the methods and resources that best suit their unique needs, whether it is through reading, watching videos, hands-on projects, adaptive technologies, or other approaches.

+ **Individualized Assessment and Feedback:** Learners are often encouraged to engage in self-assessment and reflection, helping them monitor their own progress. The learning path may also incorporate regular feedback and assessments that align with the learner's chosen goals, providing a clear picture of their achievements and areas that require improvement.

+ **Problem-solving and Critical Thinking:** This strategy strongly emphasizes problem-solving, critical thinking, and decision-making skills. While educators play a supportive role, students take a proactive stance in their education, promoting a deep sense of responsibility and accountability.

+ **Adaptation and Personal Growth:** As learners progress through a high agency learning path, they may discover new interests, change their goals, or refine their strategies. When intrinsically motivated, students are more likely to be engaged, persistent, and driven by a genuine interest in their studies.

One of the key reasons why the learning path is critical in personalized learning is its ability to address specific areas for growth and preferences. Research by Vygotsky (1978) highlights the importance of adapting instruction, emphasizing the role of scaffolding and guidance. A well-designed learning path can provide various resources and activities that cater to visual, auditory, kinesthetic, and other learning preferences, ensuring that each student can engage with the material in a way that suits them best.

The learning path empowers students to take control of their learning. In a study by Means et al. (2009), researchers found that personalized learning, focusing on allowing students to set their own pace, led to improved academic outcomes. A personalized learning path enables students to progress through the curriculum at a pace that suits their capabilities and preferences, which results in a sense of autonomy and motivation.

What makes them even more valuable is that they allow educators to adapt content. Research by Kulik and Kulik (1991) highlights that adapting instruction to individual differences can result in substantial learning gains. By customizing the learning path to each student's strengths and weaknesses, educators can provide targeted resources and activities to enhance understanding and retention. These can incorporate continuous assessment and feedback mechanisms, which play a pivotal role in learning. Research by Hattie and Timperley (2007) suggests that feedback is one of the most potent influences on learning. Personalized learning paths can provide real-time feedback on students' progress, helping them identify areas for improvement and guiding them toward mastery.

As mentioned earlier in this chapter, every student learns at their own pace, and personalized learning paths are designed to accommodate this variation. Research by Bloom (1984) demonstrated the benefits of mastery learning, a concept closely related to personalized learning, in which students must achieve a predetermined level of proficiency before progressing. Learning paths can ensure that students have mastered a topic before moving on, preventing gaps in understanding.

Here are some practical implementation strategies that allow students to follow a path aligned with their learning needs and interests:

1. Adaptive technologies
2. Choice activities (must-do/may-do tasks, choice boards, etc.)
3. Playlists
4. Self-paced learning (flipped lessons, virtual courses)
5. School-within-a-school models (academies, smaller learning communities)

Path recognizes the learner as an active participant in their educational journey. It leverages their autonomy, choice, and self-direction to create a personalized and highly engaging learning experience. This approach improves academic success and equips individuals with essential competencies and a mindset for continued self-directed learning.

Anywhere Learning

Education has undergone a remarkable transformation in recent years, and one of the most significant developments is the concept of "anywhere learning." This innovative approach to personalized education leverages technology to give students the flexibility and freedom to learn not only at their own pace, but also in their own space. Anywhere learning is proving to be a game-changer, benefiting students in many ways, primarily because it is entirely learner-centric.

First, the ability to learn anytime, anywhere, and with anyone benefits students by offering unparalleled flexibility. Traditional classroom-based education often constrains students with fixed schedules and locations. However, with anywhere learning, students can choose when and where they engage with their coursework. This flexibility allows them to adapt their learning at the individual level or to accommodate lifestyles. Whether a student is a night owl, a morning person, or has a part-time job, anywhere learning enables them to create a personalized learning schedule.

Moreover, it is particularly beneficial for students with specific learning preferences. Anywhere learning provides a wide range of resources and materials, including videos, interactive simulations, and written content, enabling students to choose the format that best suits their learning preferences. Additionally, learning anytime and anywhere develops self-discipline and time management competencies, which are crucial for students' future success. They must set goals, prioritize tasks, and establish routines to succeed. These competencies serve them well in their academic pursuits and prepare them for the demands of the modern workforce, where time management is a valuable asset. With a personalized focus, educators can create lessons, tasks, or even courses that empower students to make the most of where and when they learn.

Another significant advantage of anywhere learning is its accessibility. It breaks down geographical barriers and educates students who may need access to quality schools or universities. This democratization of education is a powerful force in promoting inclusivity and equal opportunity. Whether a student lives in a remote area, has physical disabilities, or wants to explore a curriculum not offered locally, personalization opens the doors to a world of knowledge and virtual experiences.

Furthermore, anywhere learning offers a global perspective. Students can engage with peers and educators from different backgrounds, enriching their understanding of other cultures and viewpoints. Online discussion forums and collaborative projects facilitate interactions that transcend geographical boundaries. This exposure to various perspectives is an invaluable aspect of a well-rounded education, preparing students for a globalized society.

Effective implementation requires careful planning, the right tools, and a supportive environment. Here are some suggestions on integrating anywhere learning options as a pathway to personalization:

1. **Ensure Clarity:** Establish clear learning targets by unpacking the standards that will be addressed. What are the learning goals you want to achieve? A well-defined purpose will guide your implementation strategy and help students stay on task.

2. **Select Appropriate Technology:** Choose the tools and platforms that align with your educational goals. Ensure they are user-friendly and secure and offer the features needed for various learning activities, such as video conferencing, discussion boards, and content delivery.

3. **Curriculum Development:** Adapt and create educational content suitable for online, hybrid, or remote learning. This might involve reformatting existing materials or creating new resources that engage students in an online environment. Work to maintain quality standards for content and teaching methods. Regularly review and update course materials to keep them relevant and effective.

4. **Assessment Strategies:** Design effective assessment methods that work in an online context. Assessments should align with learning objectives and be easily administered and graded digitally.

5. **Access to Devices and Internet:** Verify that students have access to the necessary devices (computers, tablets, etc.) and a reliable internet connection. Consider providing assistance or resources for students who lack access to these essentials. Ensure that student data is protected and that the online environment is secure. Implement robust data privacy and security measures to comply with regulations and safeguard sensitive information.

6. **Interactive Learning Opportunities:** Create opportunities for interaction, collaboration, and discussion. Engage students through asynchronous videos, discussion boards, group projects, and other interactive methods to encourage active learning and peer-to-peer interaction.

7. **Feedback Mechanisms:** Set up mechanisms for collecting feedback from students and educators. Regular surveys and feedback sessions can help identify issues and areas for improvement.

8. **Monitoring and Evaluation:** Continuously monitor for effectiveness. Analyze data on student performance and engagement to make informed adjustments and improvements.

9. **Communication:** Establish clear communication channels to keep students, parents, and educators informed about changes, updates, and essential information related to this means of personalization. Communicate with parents and caregivers to involve them in the learning process, especially for younger students. Provide them with information on supporting their children in an online learning environment.

10. **Flexibility and Adaptability:** Be ready to adapt and evolve this pedagogical strategy as technology advances and educational needs change. Embrace innovation and explore new opportunities as they arise.

Anywhere learning is a transformative approach to education that benefits students in numerous ways. Its flexibility, adaptability, promotion of self-discipline and time management, accessibility, global perspective, and emphasis on continuous learning make it an ideal choice for modern students. Anywhere learning empowers students to take control of their education, enabling them to thrive in a dynamic and interconnected world. As technology advances, the potential for personalization to positively impact the educational landscape and students' lives is boundless.

The Pivotal Role of Place

The physical and virtual environments in which learning takes place play a pivotal role in shaping the effectiveness and depth of personalized learning strategies. Consider for a moment the impact of the physical classroom. It is not merely a backdrop but an instrumental element that impacts learning. The arrangement of desks, collaborative spaces, and the infusion of technology all contribute to the atmosphere that shapes a student's educational experience.

Research consistently underscores the profound impact of physical and virtual learning environments on educational outcomes. According to a study by Tanner and Lackney (2006), the design of physical spaces significantly influences student engagement and academic performance. Flexible seating arrangements, varied learning zones, and interactive elements have been found to correlate positively with increased student motivation and collaboration (Tanner & Lackney, 2006). Furthermore, research by Hattie (2012) emphasizes the importance of creating a positive classroom climate, asserting that the physical layout plays a crucial role in a conducive atmosphere for learning. The influence of virtual learning environments cannot be ignored either. A Means et al. (2013) meta-analysis highlighted the importance of well-designed online platforms, emphasizing their impact on student achievement and satisfaction. As the digital landscape evolves, understanding and optimizing physical and virtual learning spaces is vital for educational success (Means et al., 2013; Hattie, 2012; Tanner & Lackney, 2006).

Physical Learning Spaces

The traditional classroom setup, with rows of desks facing forward, may not be the most conducive environment for personalized learning. Flexible seating arrangements, breakout spaces, and interactive learning corners empower students to take control of their learning. Recognizing that each student is unique, physical spaces can be designed to cater to various learning preferences, whether it be quiet individual study, collaborative group work, or hands-on experimentation.

Virtual Learning Environments

In our digital age, the concept of place extends beyond physical boundaries. Virtual learning environments, online platforms, and educational apps contribute to the personalized learning ecosystem. The design of these digital spaces, from user interface to interactive features, can significantly influence the engagement and success of personalized learning initiatives. Thoughtful consideration must be given to user experience and accessibility, ensuring the virtual place complements and enhances learning.

Research on designing effective virtual learning environments for K-12 students emphasizes creating strategies that cater to various learning profiles and utilize online pedagogical reasoning. The focus is on developing a sense of belonging in online learning, accommodating students with learning disabilities, implementing universal learning design, and promoting inclusion. These practices support K-12 education in virtual settings by providing a comprehensive framework for teachers to enhance student engagement and learning outcomes (Niess & Gillow-Wiles, 2021).

Outdoor Areas

The importance of outdoor spaces for learning cannot be overstated, as they offer a transformative and holistic dimension to education. Beyond the traditional confines of classrooms, the outdoors provides a dynamic setting that stimulates curiosity, creativity, and a sense of exploration. Nature becomes an influential teacher, offering biology, ecology, and environmental science lessons in a living laboratory. Beyond academic subjects, outdoor spaces promote physical activity, contributing to students' overall well-being. The fresh air and natural light create a stimulating atmosphere that improves focus and reduces stress. Moreover, outdoor environments encourage collaboration, teamwork, and social skills as students engage in activities that often require cooperation and communication. Educators enrich the academic curriculum by integrating outdoor spaces into the learning experience and cultivating a love for the environment and a deeper connection to the world around us.

Here are some specific strategies for crafting effective learning spaces:

- **Individualized Learning Zones:** Create individualized learning zones to break traditional classroom barriers. Students can have a designated space that aligns with their preferred learning preference, such as a quiet corner for reflection or an interactive area for hands-on exploration.
- **Technology Integration:** Leverage technology to bridge the physical and virtual learning spaces. Interactive whiteboards, digital collaboration tools, and online resources can seamlessly integrate into the classroom, providing a dynamic and personalized learning experience.
- **Flexible Furniture:** The days of static desks and chairs are behind us. Embrace flexible furniture that can be easily rearranged to accommodate different learning activities. This adaptability promotes a sense of ownership over the learning environment.
- **Makerspaces:** These represent a place for learners to collaborate, hack, invent, share, create, make, and do, which is the epitome of personalization. It is about creating a genuine commitment to innovation that encourages tinkering, play, and open-ended exploration for all students. The premise is simple: allow students to utilize guided inquiry in an informal learning

environment facilitated using real-world tools to do real-world work. Students can actively explore their passions while learning from failure and trial and error.

+ **Student-Centric Design:** Involve students in the design process. Solicit their input on the classroom layout, the choice of furniture, and technology integration. A student-centric approach ensures that the learning space truly resonates with its inhabitants.

As you embark on the personalized learning campaign, consider the impact of place. The physical, outdoor, and virtual environments in which learning unfolds are not passive backdrops but active participants in the educational process. By strategically crafting these spaces, we can amplify the effectiveness of personalized learning. The power of place extends beyond the confines of walls and screens; it is a dynamic force shaping the essence of how we learn and grow.

A Student Perspective

Many years ago, I (Eric) was sitting in my office when sophomore Sarah Almeda popped into my office, as usual. After day three of standardized testing, I was catching up on some dreaded paperwork, one of the least favorite aspects of my job. Sarah asked if she could email me her presentation as part of the Academies program, a school-within-a-school model, at New Milford High School (NJ). I said sure but then asked her when she would give the presentation. Her reply was later that day. I immediately looked at my calendar, cleared the time, and told her there was no need to email the presentation to me as I was going to attend in person.

As part of our Academies program, students engaged in authentic learning activities outside the school day through field trips or special projects. These were in addition to the added coursework required for an Academies designation. For this particular activity, students had to read *Out of Our Minds: Learning to Be Creative* by Ken Robinson. They then watched a video and had to create a presentation, with each student sharing their "creative" experiences with the group. Total freedom was given to create a presentation in any format they wanted to include, but not limited to a written document, a poster, a collage, a pinboard, a chart, etc. Each student had to be prepared to answer and explain the items below:

+ Tell the group about your creative self. Explain how you are creative (what is your medium?).
+ Describe when you feel the most inspired.
+ Explain what stifles your creativity.
+ Tell us about (at least) one person whose creativity you admire and how they inspire you.
+ Explain what you believe schools need to do better to promote and enhance students' creativity. Provide an example of something that would have helped you be more creative or something/someone who did help you.

Now, back to Sarah. After watching some fantastic presentations, Sarah's turn came. I had to use my administrative privileges to get the YouTube video to work for her. Once her video began, everyone was floored. I can honestly say that this was one of the best, most inspiring, thought-provoking student presentations I have ever seen. It was created entirely through self-directed learning and sent a strong message about how powerful creativity is for our students and how high-agency strategies are embraced. She made her final product using an array of digital tools and ingenuity. You can view the video of the project at youtu.be/jHHhTRAZARM

Personalization matters to students. It affirms what they want and need in education and how we can strive to make it happen.

Throughout the presentations, I heard student after student discuss how vital agency is regarding creativity and their learning. Their words expressed how they yearned to have freedom over demonstrating what they know and a genuine desire to have ownership of their learning.

As Sarah's story shows, students shine when given the autonomy to produce a learning artifact that is meaningful, relevant, and reflects the importance of voice, choice, path, pace, and place. Regarding creativity and learning, standardized tests are one of the most significant inhibitors. While these play a role in the trajectory of our learners, an emphasis on high-agency personalization will unlock potential while preparing them for future success. Do not prepare students for something. Prepare them for anything.

Think back to the story of Mary that we shared in the introduction. As she explained, tailoring learning to each student precisely when and where they are ready to learn is rewarding and has a lasting impact. Personalization through high-agency practices makes this a reality. Just like Mary's teacher profoundly influenced her, you can have the same impact on your students.

Bold Moves

Personalization represents a paradigm shift in education by implementing high-agency strategies that prioritize learning through choice, voice, path, place, and place. Educators are encouraged to adopt a "free-range" approach, allowing students to have greater ownership of their learning through active involvement during lessons, choosing tasks and setting their own goals, thereby increasing engagement and intrinsic motivation. With an emphasis on student-driven learning, educators can implement practical methods such as must-do/may-do activities, choice boards, flipped lessons, and playlists, which empower students to take charge of their educational paths. Appendix 2 contains an array of examples showing high-agency practices in K-12 classrooms.

Educators must also redesign physical and virtual learning spaces to support these high-agency strategies. They can create inclusive environments that cater to diverse learning preferences and needs by employing technology and flexible pedagogies. This approach encourages students to take responsibility for their learning and equips them with critical life competencies such as problem-solving, decision-making, and self-regulation. By transitioning from a one-size-fits-all model to a personalized learning experience, educators can enable students to thrive in an ever-evolving world.

Bold moves require taking risks. This means questioning how you've always done things and finding new ways to grow, even if it challenges the status quo or your past experience. The following questions will help you on this quest.

1. How can I modify my practices to promote a "free-range" learning environment that allows students to pursue their interests within a structured framework?
2. How can I integrate choice boards, playlists, flipped lessons, and must-do/may-do activities to offer students more control over their learning process?
3. What steps can I take to reconfigure my classroom's physical and virtual learning spaces to support individualized learning better?
4. How can I effectively transfer some of the responsibility for learning from myself to my students in a supportive way that promotes their autonomy and accountability?
5. What effective strategies can I employ to honor my students' voices and genuinely incorporate their feedback into the learning environment?

Share your progress on social media (Instagram, Twitter, LinkedIn, Facebook, TikTok) using the **#personalize** hashtag.

CHAPTER 4

Proof of Learning

Teachers often graded my academic performance based on the completion of assignments. Even if I didn't grasp the content, I could receive points if I was compliant, took notes, or submitted work on time. When I was absent, I would copy my friends' notes, playing the system to secure the A. It wasn't about understanding the questions on the worksheet but about turning it in on time. I had never heard of the terms learning targets, reteaching, or feedback. The only focus was accumulating points. It was hard to feel like I was learning the material when we were always moving on despite my scores.

The story above depicts a need to examine how grades reflect learning and what motivates students. When I (Nicki) decided to transition from points to learning, the first task was to develop a measurement tool for our students. As educators, we want to be clear and transparent about our learning targets. Before developing rubric scales, a possible starting point is to interview students of all ages to determine their perceptions of "points." and pose questions such as: What are you learning? Why are you learning it? How do you determine your understanding of the material? How does your teacher assess your success? Throughout these conversations, you might find several noteworthy statements begin to emerge.

For example, students frequently associated success with the timely submission of assignments. Many expressed a disconnect between their classroom activities and the content assessed, needing help to discern what to prepare for in assessments. It was common for them to study their notes only to find that assessments covered unrelated material. The numerical representation, such as 18/25, merely reflected the number of correct answers without truly capturing their comprehension.

Older students described school as a game where they meticulously calculated points throughout the quarter to ensure they achieved the required amount for an A. When asked about the consequences of not earning the total points on an assignment or assessment, they calmly replied that they moved on, emphasizing that the cumulative total of points at the end of the quarter was all that mattered.

When engaging in discussions with younger students about their preference for teachers using rubrics instead of solely assigning scores to their assignments, they shared insightful responses:

- "It helps me understand exactly what I need to do."
- "I enjoy the visual cues like pictures and symbols that indicate my performance."
- "Rubrics make it clearer for me to grasp what is expected of me."
- "I can identify my strengths and areas for improvement."

Based on these conversations, many students at all age levels see the value in rubrics over points for their clarity, visual aids, constructive feedback, and the sense of accomplishment they bring, enhancing the structured and engaging nature of learning experiences.

Students should view learning as a lifelong competency; it was time for a change at our school. Contemplating how to facilitate collaboration between students and teachers, we envisioned an idea with elevated expectations where students had to demonstrate understanding before advancing. The aspiration was for students to perceive errors as opportunities for growth, to create a space that advanced meaningful one-on-one interactions, and to establish constructive feedback as the new standard when assessing students. It was determined that something was missing; students needed more clarity and meaning in their learning.

Moving from Skills to Competencies

The dialogue around the skills necessary for success will always be a topic of conversation. These discussions have spurred teachers, schools, districts, and various organizations to examine the knowledge students require to thrive in the evolving disruptive landscape. As we have advanced deeper into this century, how we label skills may have diminished in specificity, but the importance of these skills endures. Consequently, many in the educational field, ourselves included, have come to describe these as "essential skills." Over time, this skill set has expanded to include communication, collaboration, creativity, global consciousness, entrepreneurial aptitude, and proficiency in new and developing technologies.

While acquiring skills is vital to education and career development, they alone are insufficient for guiding students to true proficiency and achievement. Here is where personalization changes the emphasis from "schooling" to learning. Skills are about the "what"—the specific abilities a student must have to perform certain tasks. However, they lack a thorough connection to the "how" of the application. Competencies expand upon this, transforming skills into observable behaviors that provide tangible evidence of learning and mastery. Essentially, while skills point to objectives to be met, competencies delineate *how* these objectives will be achieved, encapsulating a richer and more holistic definition of success criteria.

Competencies encompass a skillset, depth of understanding and behavior that signify an individual's capacity to apply what they have learned effectively. For example, a student's ability to thrive in today's work environment depends on a harmonious blend of skills, knowledge, and practical application. A skill might demonstrate a student's ability to perform a task, but competency is the application of skills, knowledge, and abilities in problem-solving, showcasing a mastery of the learning process.

The distinction between a skill and a competency can be illustrated by considering presentation abilities versus communication competencies. One may learn to present well through practice and education. Still, strong communication requires a synergy of skills, behavior, and knowledge, such as advanced language skills, cultural understanding, and the ability to engage patiently. While skills might be isolated actions like typing or data entry, competencies are more complex, integrating skills with relevant knowledge and appropriate behaviors—like critical thinking, effective communication, or demonstrating professionalism. Competencies are dynamic, combining abilities, attitudes, behaviors, and knowledge fundamental to effectively applying a skill in different situations.

Personalized learning strategies extend beyond skill development, focusing on a full exploration that aligns with each student's unique learning path. This educational approach is not merely about acquiring specific abilities but about shaping learners into individuals who can navigate and adapt to an ever-evolving landscape through a deepened self-awareness and intrinsic motivation. There is a more profound emphasis on creating learner profiles that capture the distinction of each student's strengths, needs, and aspirations, thereby improving individual achievement and growth. By allowing students to engage with content through personalized learning pathways and competency-based progression, this approach addresses the whole student, considering their personal development, well-being, and engagement as part of the learning process.

Educational frameworks like the Relevant Thinking Framework, presented in Chapter 2, support the move from a focus on skills to competency-based learning. The framework encourages integrating and applying concepts to address real-world challenges. This approach underscores cognitive growth while enhancing motivation and the relevance of learning. Moreover, increased autonomy in personalized learning environments empowers students to take control of their educational journey through self-regulation and independence, key competencies in navigating future uncertainties.

Succeeding in a disruptive world demands more than mere skills—it emphasizes nurturing, evaluating, and unpacking competencies that will equip students for present and future challenges.

Sensibility of Unpacking

Surprisingly, many educators often engage in a random review of the standards and associated competencies, relying only on the prescribed curriculum for instruction. Unfortunately, unpacking standards—determining what students need to know, identifying key nouns and verbs, and vertically aligning with adjacent grade levels—is not as widespread as it should be. In the context of a personalized learning environment, understanding not only your grade-level standards but also those above and below is indispensable in defining the parameters of student success.

Once you have unpacked your grade-level standards, it is time to pose a fundamental question: What standards are necessary for my students to learn to demonstrate success this academic year? Collaborate with your teaching teams to decide the essential standards for mastery at each grade level, emphasizing quality over quantity. These become your power standards. Teacher teams must identify and understand the power standards and then build backward from there (Wiggins & McTighe, 2005). Power standards are those standards that are critical to students' success (Ainsworth, 2003). Change the mindset from covering the entire curriculum to ensuring students truly learn and master what is essential to know.

According to Marzano (2003), teachers who increased their understanding of competencies about standards ensured a guaranteed and viable curriculum, a curriculum that (1) gives students access to the same essential learning regardless of who is teaching the class and (2) can be taught in the time allotted. Once power standards are selected, examine each and identify the nouns and verbs. Nouns typically indicate what students need to know, while verbs articulate the skills students must acquire to establish connections and learn effectively.

This phase initiates a transformative process, igniting discussions among teams focused on learning. It entails evaluating the alignment of current assessments with the standards, delving into each standard to pinpoint essential learning progressions for mastery. Commonly known as "unpacking" the standard, this process entails backward planning, commencing with the desired targeted outcome, and exploring various ways students can demonstrate mastery. When collaboratively "unpacking" standards, teachers work together to design meaningful learning experiences, guiding students toward proficiency. Their role becomes purposeful and meaningful as they operate behind the scenes as professionals in the craft of teaching.

You will naturally begin to detect which "learning progressions" are vital in establishing pathways to proficiency—think of them as signposts along the way, guiding the way to mastery. To gauge student success, teachers must articulate what the success criteria entails. Often withheld from students, this clarity serves as the road map to the final destination, offering transparency and removing guesswork from the educational process. The educator guides, mentors, and coaches students in their learning journey, emphasizing guidance over deceit or punishment.

Consider the success criteria as the roadmap guiding them to mastery or demonstrating understanding. When establishing this criterion, ensure clarity, actionability, and the ability to enable self-assessment,

thereby enhancing student motivation. For students to be active participants, they must be able to identify what they are learning, why they
are learning it, and how they are progressing.

Another critical aspect of this process is dedicating time to determine when and how to assess understanding. This involves adapting
to the pace at which students grasp concepts or the need for alternative teaching methods. All these steps form the foundational building
blocks of rubric creation. Through this intentional process, educators
gain confidence in their teaching roles. They begin to perceive themselves as architects of their students' learning experiences, familiarizing
themselves with the prerequisites and subsequent expectations for each
grade level in a personalized learning environment.

Creating Effective Rubrics

Rubrics emerge as invaluable tools in the relentless pursuit of student
mastery, empowering educators and students to navigate the curriculum with clarity and purpose. The traditional, often opaque, grading
process is transformed into a dynamic and engaging experience by
opting for rubrics. Educators benefit from clear evaluation criteria,
streamlining the grading process and allowing for more focused feedback (Popham, 2008). Students, empowered by the transparency of
rubrics, can actively track their progress toward learning goals, engage
in self-assessment, and become partners in their learning journey
(Moss & Brookhart, 2001).

This shift promotes an environment where feedback becomes a conversation, not a judgment, and strengthens the relationships between
students and teachers. Rubrics become a bridge of mutual understanding, trust, and a shared commitment to growth. Implementing rubrics
transcends mere assessment, weaving a transparent picture of engaged
learning, empowered students, and a collaborative learning environment
where all stakeholders actively contribute to the pursuit of mastery.

To use rubrics effectively, begin by clearly articulating the standards and learning objectives you intend your students of all ages to understand, demonstrate, or achieve. Selecting one that aligns with your classroom or school context becomes your responsibility. The subsequent step involves crafting the layout, with various rubric versions available. Organize your rubric in a clear and easy-to-follow structure, possibly using a table format with criteria listed vertically and performance levels horizontally. Once the template is in place, establish distinct performance levels for each criterion. Detailing each criterion and performance level with specific language and examples enhances clarity for both students and assessors.

Use action verbs to convey the expected performance at each level, rendering the rubric more actionable and guiding students in comprehending the steps necessary to attain a specific learning level. It is imperative to clearly define the system, ensuring alignment with grading policies, whether it involves a numerical scale, letter grades, or a pass/fail system.

Most importantly, include designated spaces for teacher feedback and a self-reflection area for students to assess their learning. This addition facilitates constructive feedback and promotes self-awareness and a sense of ownership in the learning process. By incorporating these elements, your rubric becomes a comprehensive tool that assesses performance and serves as a tool for continuous improvement and a deeper understanding of learning objectives. Reminders for an effective rubric:

+ Be descriptive, not vague.
+ Quantity does not equal quality.
+ Do not include "what is missing". Use "I Can" positive wording instead.
+ Criteria should consist of both foundational understandings and deeper thinking.
+ Use the Relevant Thinking Framework to guide you.

- Be kid friendly.
- Focus on the quality of student work.
- Create extension opportunities.

In pursuing effective teaching and learning practices, rubrics provide clarity and empowerment for educators and students. As educators embrace the transformative power, they are equipped with invaluable tools that streamline the grading process, provide clear evaluation criteria, and offer meaningful feedback. Simultaneously, students are empowered by the transparency of rubrics, enabling them to actively track their progress, engage in self-assessment, and take ownership of their education. Moving from traditional grading methods to rubric-based assessment cultivates collaboration, trust, and mutual understanding between students and teachers.

John Hattie's (2009) research on teacher clarity suggests that it substantially affects student learning outcomes. The effect size for teacher clarity is reported to be around 0.75, considered high according to Hattie's criteria. In this context, an effect size of 0.75 indicates that when teachers demonstrate clarity in their instruction, it significantly impacts student learning. Teacher clarity refers to the ability of educators to communicate learning goals, provide explicit instructions, offer understandable explanations, and provide feedback that helps students understand their progress. When teachers are clear in their communication and instruction, students are more likely to comprehend the material, engage in learning tasks, and achieve academic success. Rubrics are an easy way to provide teacher clarity.

Rubrics serve as bridges that connect learners and educators to a shared commitment to growth and mastery. Beyond mere assessment tools, rubrics portray a more realistic view of engaged learning, empowered students, and collaborative environments in which all stakeholders actively contribute to the pursuit of excellence. Thus, by embracing the principles of effective rubric creation and implementation, educators pave the way for enriched teaching and learning experiences that transcend conventional boundaries and empower individuals to reach their fullest potential. Appendix 3 provides K-12 rubric examples.

Quality Over Quantity

There has been a longstanding tendency to prioritize easily quantifiable metrics over those that truly reflect the essence of educational progress. Instead of serving as catalysts for meaningful action, these data points often serve as superficial markers of achievement, needing more context and nuance. It is vital to understand that a single data point cannot capture the complexities of a student's learning journey.

Moreover, the prevailing approach of strictly adhering to state standards or a uniform curriculum overlooks individuality and experiences. Simply meeting administrative requirements does not ensure genuine educational attainment or student engagement; it merely scratches the surface of objectives. So, what alternative approach should we embrace? We advocate for a shift from quantity to quality—a methodology prioritizing actionable, timely, and student-centered data points. Considering multiple indicators relevant to each student, we can paint a more comprehensive picture of educational progress. We can personalize the learning for all.

The traditional teaching model often prioritizes quantity over quality, rushing through curriculum at the expense of true comprehension and mastery. However, transitioning towards a quality-over-quantity approach is crucial for meaningful learning at all levels. Instead of merely checking off boxes to indicate that a lesson has been taught, educators should focus on cultivating a deep understanding and mastery of standards. This requires moving away from rigid adherence to textbooks and "canned" curriculum towards a more user-centered approach that recognizes the individual. By embracing personalized pathways for learning, educators can better address each student's unique strengths and challenges, ensuring that no one falls through the cracks.

Meaningful assessment data plays a crucial role in this approach, which will be detailed in Chapter 5. It provides educators with valuable insights into student progress and enables them to tailor instruction accordingly. Our primary goal as educators should be to facilitate genuine learning experiences that empower students to succeed, regardless of their starting point or level of proficiency.

In essence, measurement matters, but only when aligned with the true objectives of education. We must recalibrate our data collection approach to ensure we measure the right things for our school communities. We need a measurement system that empowers educators to enact targeted interventions for authentic student growth. When schools prioritize quality over quantity, they will obtain the data required to support growth and create personalized pathways for their students. Consider this: What is the benefit of teaching with a cookie-cutter curriculum and exposing students to information without ensuring they learn? Or using the same measurement tool that only provides a single data point? Too often, students are overlooked or rushed through the system, receiving passing grades without genuinely mastering the material. Unfortunately, this is an example of quantity over quality.

Effective data collection is essential for personalizing learning within a school. By gathering comprehensive and relevant data points, educators gain insights into each student's strengths, weaknesses, and unique learning preferences. This information allows teachers to offer differentiated learning experiences that cater to individual preferences and abilities. Some key considerations for data collection include:

+ Understanding the tools teachers and students utilize in classrooms.
+ Determining the data types gathered by these tools and their potential to guide future actions for students and educators.
+ Assessing the significance of collected data and eliminating irrelevant information to concentrate on essentials.
+ Recognizing gaps in data and devising methods to acquire pertinent, timely, and meaningful information.

Once these considerations are addressed, it is time to adopt a user-centered approach to data collection. This begins with an annual baseline survey to establish benchmarks and identify critical trends. Questions should be designed in collaboration with a team, resembling "check for understanding" checkpoints for the core curriculum. Additionally, a "pulse assessment" measuring the well-being, engagement, and satisfaction of both teachers and students is crucial. This data should offer real-time snapshots of what is happening in the school or classroom and should be seamlessly integrated into existing processes within the school community.

Proof of Understanding

When I (Nicki) was a teacher in the classroom, I did not use assignments as part of the final grade. Later, as an administrator, I trained teachers the same way. Assignments are like the ingredients and preparation steps when cooking dinner for your family, allowing students to practice and hone their skills. The final test would assess the dish you serve. The tests you choose to evaluate your students are the ultimate evaluation, ensuring that students have the ingredients, know the steps, and can apply their knowledge effectively under pressure, just like a chef showcasing their culinary expertise in the kitchen. Several educational principles support the idea of using assignments for practice and feedback:

Formative Assessment: Formative assessment, which includes assignments, exit tickets and observations, is intended to provide feedback to students on their learning progress rather than assigning grades. It can have a profound impact on student learning outcomes. Unlike summative evaluation, formative assessment is an ongoing process providing timely feedback to teachers and students, aiding instructional decisions. By integrating formative assessment practices into instruction and delivering specific, actionable feedback, teachers can better understand students' progress, address gaps promptly, and create a more supportive learning environment conducive to enhanced learning outcomes.

Learning for Mastery: Focusing on assignments as practice aligns with the concept of mastery learning, which emphasizes the importance of giving students ample time and support to fully master content at their own pace before moving on to more advanced topics. In a standards-based grading system, students must demonstrate a high-level understanding of each standard before moving to the next concept. Allowing students to practice without the pressure of grades can lead to deeper understanding and better knowledge retention. This student-centered approach prioritizes personalized instruction and continuous assessment, coupled with formative feedback, enabling students to build a solid understanding foundation and enhance learning outcomes.

Focus on Feedback: John Hattie (2009) highlights the transformative power of replacing graded assignments with meaningful feedback.

Effective feedback plays a pivotal role in shaping student learning and achievement. By offering specific, actionable feedback highlighting strengths and areas for improvement, teachers can guide students toward a deeper understanding and mastery of content. Hattie's work (2009) emphasizes that feedback is most impactful when it is timely, relevant, and focused on learning goals. When students receive such feedback, they can adjust their learning strategies. By prioritizing feedback over grades, educators can cultivate a supportive learning environment in which students are empowered to take ownership of their learning and strive for continuous improvement.

As a principal, I developed the practice, practice, practice, prove method. All practices are preparation to prove understanding. Verbiage is critical for student embracement and engagement. A simple switch in calling students "learners," assignments "practices," and assessments "prove its" can make a massive difference within your school or classroom. When you use technology resources to receive instant data while facilitating instruction, consider adding exit tickets, conducting small group and one-on-one meetings, and circulating your classroom to check for understanding. Using that information and data to be proactive ensures that your students learn what they need to prove understanding on the final assessment.

When we have guided leaders and teachers on tours to witness this method in action, they have been pleasantly surprised by students' willingness to complete assignments for the sake of learning rather than for points. This demonstrates intrinsic motivation, a crucial competency for success. By removing assignments from the formal grade book, students develop intrinsic motivation as they engage in learning for its inherent value rather than for external rewards. This intrinsic motivation improves learning outcomes and encourages sustained engagement with academic tasks over the long term. In a personalized learning environment, students guided by proficiency scales and rubrics understand that active participation in completing assignments is the key to demonstrating understanding, allowing them to progress through the standards.

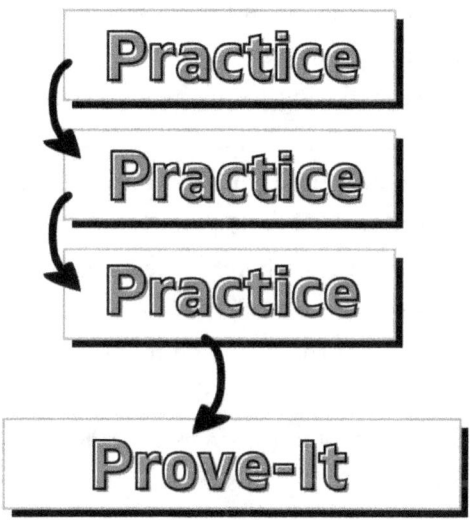

Along with developing intrinsic motivation, removing the stress of grades from assignments decreases student anxiety. This environment cultivates a sense of safety, where students feel free from the fear of failure. It provides a welcoming space for asking questions, exploring innovative ideas, and embracing the process of learning, creating a supportive atmosphere. High levels of anxiety can hinder cognitive performance, whereas a low-stress environment can optimize learning outcomes.

Indeed, the goal is for all students to be reflective, feel confident, and be prepared to pass the assessment on the first attempt. This happens when you intentionally design practice, provide clear and transparent rubrics, and use formative assessment data to proactively reteach your students throughout the practice cycle. This method is intentional, and learning is the heart and soul. Teachers love that this work is meaningful and purposeful. They see immediate growth and learning rather than spending hours each day correcting assignments and inputting scores into a grading system. Students are also engaged and see purpose in their daily work instead of just handing in assignments to check off the box. It is a win-win for both students and teachers, with learning always at the forefront as the goal.

Remember, when choosing to follow a method such as this one, the practices serve as the controlled environment in which students can refine their techniques and build confidence, much like swimmers must practice strokes in the safety of the pool. However, just as the swimmer dives into deeper waters where the real challenges lie, a well-designed final assessment allows students to demonstrate that they have mastered the skills needed to navigate different scenarios and depths. "Prove it's" act as the final evaluation, allowing students to demonstrate their proficiency and adaptability in real-world situations, just like swimming in deeper waters requires applying learned techniques effectively to stay afloat and navigate obstacles.

Necessity of Ongoing Feedback

Feedback paired with rubrics creates a structured and transparent framework that enhances communication, aids mutual understanding, and promotes collaboration between teachers and students. It encourages shared goals, continuous improvement, and respect within the educational relationship. This framework's transparency enables students to comprehend expectations and understand how their work will be assessed. When students clearly understand grading criteria, the teacher-student relationship is strengthened through fairness and transparency.

It is crucial to be proactive to optimize our students' learning experience. Instead of waiting until students submit their final projects or assessments and evaluating them using a rubric, consider integrating rubrics as daily guides. Using the rubric, incorporate tasks that prompt students to self-assess their work daily. This approach diverges from the conventional method, where a score is given, and students move on to the following standard without sufficient time for feedback. We gather valuable data and a more robust understanding of the learning process by employing rubrics as ongoing guides. Encouraging self-assessment, conferences, and formative assessments along the learning process helps students learn how to learn and glean insights from their mistakes.

The continuous exchange of feedback between students and teachers creates a personalized learning experience. This personalized approach ensures that students receive the necessary support to demonstrate understanding the first time. Proactively meeting individual needs throughout the learning process is crucial for developing lifelong learners and provides the mastery of standards.

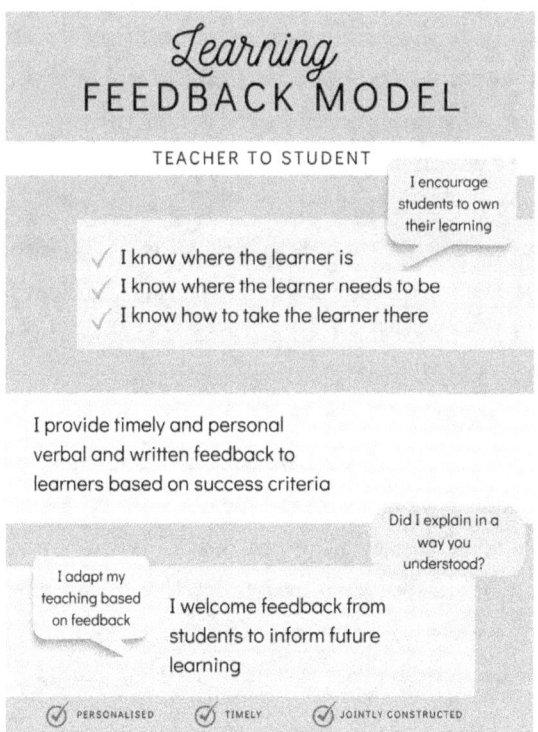

The Power of Reteaching

When allowed to self-reflect as an educator, it is easy to realize the profound importance of reteaching in the classroom. Early on, as educators, we are often asked to create our "why"—our teaching philosophy. However, when teachers start their careers, the pressures of the curriculum and the ever-ticking clock to cover everything begins. Often, teachers are caught up in the rush to complete the syllabus, use a set curriculum, and, in so doing, inadvertently overlook their profession's fundamental essence to facilitate learning and understanding. Our why tends to get lost in the hustle and bustle of our everyday lives as educators, just checking off boxes to survive.

Take time to ask yourself: "Are we truly doing justice to our students if we are merely racing through the curriculum without ensuring they genuinely understand the material?" This question hangs in the air and is a critical issue. Another question to ponder: "If a student cannot prove their understanding on an assessment, isn't it our responsibility to provide them with an opportunity to bridge the gaps in their knowledge? Shouldn't we offer a second chance—a reteach, if you will—to help them grasp the concept better?" The answer is YES!

We must realize that our ultimate goal is not just to teach but to instill a thirst for knowledge and ensure each student's comprehension. Wouldn't it be nice if we all pledged to devote time and effort to reteaching, acknowledging that it is essential to student success? The answer is YES again!

Think about it: Learning is the core of our profession. Where did the learning occur if we just let students submit work and move on, no matter the outcome? Reteaching not only aids students in cultivating the mentioned habits but also assists in developing meaningful relationships with your students, where it is acceptable to experience failure and where learning happens amidst the challenges.

Within a personalized learning environment focusing on path, pace, place, voice, and choice, there are multiple opportunities to give formative assessments, check for understanding, and self-reflection. All these systematic strategies allow you to be proactive in your student's learning process. When using data from formative assessment options, you can reteach specific content before they take the final assessment. The goal is always to pass the assessment with understanding the first time. However, if a student does not pass, you must build in time for a reteach, additional practice, and then time for your students to retake the assessment.

Some secondary schools have a flex period or study hall during the day where students can work on missing assignments. Instead of using that time for missing work, use that time for scheduled reteach sessions with the core teachers. This could be integrated into station rotation or center time in elementary schools. If you want to find time during class to reteach your students, move away from the teacher-centered approach with the teacher lecturing in front of the room to more of a student-centered approach where the teacher has time to circulate, meet one one-on-one or meet in small groups because they have set up their class where they do not have to be doing all of the talking the entire class period. Once you build in time for reteaching to happen, this practice promotes the importance of learning with high expectations, and it shows that you value your students as individuals and want them to succeed.

Do not underestimate the power of reteaching. Reteaching is a tool for identifying and bridging gaps while offering additional explanations and examples. It also serves as a method for reinforcing critical concepts across various subjects. The reiteration solidifies these ideas in the students' memory, making it easier for them to apply these concepts to more complex learning scenarios in the future. Reteaching does not just focus on short-term memorization for exams; it aims for long-term knowledge retention. The learning becomes an ongoing process, a route towards an understanding beyond test scores. That is the goal: to create lifelong learners in our classrooms.

Beyond academics, reteaching becomes a confidence booster. Students who once struggled with concepts found their self-assurance growing as they mastered previously challenging material. It was not just about understanding the subject but about instilling a learning mindset that encouraged them to take on new challenges with new-found confidence.

A teacher once told me about when she had a new student, a young boy named Charlie, who struggled with mathematics. No matter how he tried, he could not grasp the concepts presented in class. The teacher noticed Charlie's determination and frustration. She knew he had potential and was determined to identify how he learns best and provide a more personalized experience.

She started to implement the re-teach. Instead of allowing him to keep slipping through the cracks at, say, a C average at each assessment, she decided to take time to re-teach him a different way than was initially taught. Through these one-on-one meetings, she learned how he learns best, using visual aids, real-life examples, and analogies to help him understand. She also created a trusting relationship with Charlie. Charlie started to feel safe in her classroom. He was no longer afraid to ask questions and knew his teacher would have his back. Charlie's confidence grew, and he stopped dreading math class.

The power of a re-teach changed Charlie's life. He became a passionate learner and took time to identify when he was struggling and fight through his comfort zone. Not only did this teacher change his mindset in the math classroom, but she also impacted all future challenges he may encounter. This is just one example of why reteaching is a powerful, sometimes overlooked strategy.

Student Ownership and Tracking

For years, the educational landscape has emphasized the importance of grades, points, and percentages as the primary metrics of a student's progress. As the tides of education are veering toward a more personalized approach, a glaring rift needs to be filled. Student grade books are designed to track points and percentages, but, in a personalized learning environment, grades should be based on learning, rubrics, and feedback rather than points.

Two decades ago, during my tenure as an elementary school teacher, I (Nicki) recognized the limitations of using mere numbers or letters to assess students' knowledge. I leveraged our educational standards and crafted "I can" statements to address this. These statements clarified my expectations for students and provided parents and guardians with insights into their child's learning progress. This experience marked the beginning of my passion for standards-based grading. It enabled me to set ambitious academic goals for my students and tailor support specific to each child's needs, regardless of their starting point in my class. By embracing "I can" statements and visual aids like charts or rubrics, students at a young age took ownership of their learning. They gained a clear understanding of their progress, moving beyond traditional grading systems reliant on numbers and letters.

Seven years ago, I made another bold leap, committing myself to this transformative vision in a secondary setting. I decided to deviate from traditional grading and instead directed it toward learning and comprehension. This shift necessitated a tool that could effectively communicate each student's progress in their learning journey to both the students themselves and their parents. I yearned for a system that could report on their competencies and help them visualize their learning trajectory—months of research and experimentation proved frustrating because no existing program met my requirements. It was then that I took matters into my own hands. Armed with my vision, my past experiences as an elementary teacher using standards-based grading, and getting feedback from numerous teacher teams, I started to design a tracking tool for our students to use daily. Luckily, I found a staff member willing to embark on an initiative to learn coding and turn my dream into reality.

Together, we devised what we now call the "My Mastery Tracker" for each student, which can be viewed at bit.ly/PLbook_tracker. This tracker is for secondary schools but could also be adapted for elementary ones. This specific tracker displays each student's class schedule, highlights missing standards, provides a citizenship grade, and features an area for teachers to add their "I can" statements and competencies. The "My Mastery Tracker" was closely aligned with our Learning Process Scale, which tracked proficiencies. Rather than relying on traditional letter grades or numbers, we opted for a system to indicate whether students were emerging, developing, mastering, or extending based on each competency.

THE LEARNING PROCESS

I yearned for a streamlined, one-stop solution for students, parents, and teachers. In this place, anyone could quickly assess a student's progress in the learning process and life skills such as personal responsibility, respect, integrity, discipline, and engagement. The "My Mastery Tracker" achieves this, offering clarity and ease of understanding for all involved. It removes doubts regarding what a child is working on, whether they truly understand the material, and what citizenship characteristics they have accomplished.

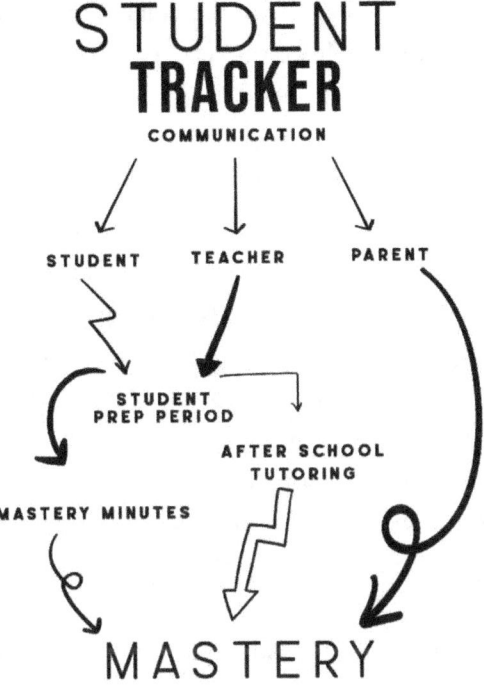

This versatile tracker serves multiple purposes, with its primary role being in our daily Student Prep Period, but it could also be used during your Morning Meeting time in an elementary setting. During this crucial 30-minute period at the start of each day, students must consult their "My Mastery Tracker." With guidance from mentors, teachers, and coaches, they determine what they need to work on or excel at. The tracker also plays a pivotal role in deciding where each student should go during our Mastery Minutes Period. Look to maximize the time that you might already have to align with your rubrics and reinforce the goal of reaching mastery for each standard. The goal of this practice is for students to have a digital tool that identifies where they are in the learning process. Then, they know exactly what to work on during a station rotation setting or a flex period, depending on the student's age. For example, suppose a student finds themselves in the emerging or developing category for a particular standard. In that case, they know it is time to seek a reteach from the teacher during the designated time in their daily schedule. Afterward, they can retake the assessment to demonstrate their understanding. The key component is to hold your students to high standards and only allow them to move on to the next standard, skill, or concept once they have proven their understanding.

Self-directed learning is often seen as a valuable skill for lifelong learning. Research suggests that students adept at tracking their learning are better equipped to take on new challenges and adapt to different learning environments beyond the classroom (Johnson & Persky, 2020). Allowing students to track their learning advances a sense of responsibility and independence. For example, research from Devi et al. (2017) indicates that students who actively manage their own learning are more likely to develop a sense of agency and take control of their learning.

Numerous studies have also explored the relationship between goal setting, student participation in the goal-setting processes, and academic achievement (Boekaerts et al., 2000; Locke & Latham, 2002; Deci & Ryan, 2008). When students proactively establish and track their own learning objectives, they can experience an enhanced sense of autonomy in their educational path, fostering a recognition of their own agency, all of which "My Mastery Tracker" allows to happen.

Consider developing a digital tool like the "My Mastery Tracker" accessible 24/7 to students, parents, and teachers. Doing so will address a critical missing piece in the educational puzzle. Many schools aspire to transition away from traditional grading, but they need a clear and transparent tracking system to ensure their progress. The "My Mastery Tracker" concept has become a valuable tool and resource for students. It is a reporting system and a means to develop learner agency and empower students to make decisions for themselves. It embodies a purpose and meaning that transcends the limitations of traditional grading systems. It is our job to provide our students with the tools to not only help with accountability but also help them set daily goals and reach their full potential. Our focus is and always will be on student learning and understanding.

Leveraging Exit Tickets

During our training to become teachers, we were both immersed in Madeline Hunter's (1994) work regarding lesson plan design. Her Instructional Theory into Practice (ITIP) model helped me (Eric) identify the strategies I would use daily to help my students learn. These included the anticipatory set (hook), reviewing prior learning, checking for understanding, forms of practice, and closure. Every lesson had these elements, and I often received positive feedback from administrators on these when they observed me. Closure is something I was incredibly proud of, and I always ended lessons with some form of paper exit ticket.

As important as the initial moments spent with students are, the concluding minutes of a lesson are equally important. Consider this notion: What purpose does an objective or learning target serve, whether explicitly stated on the board or presented for students to explore independently if there is no chance at the lesson's conclusion to assess whether it has been accomplished? The effectiveness of the learning process is enhanced when lessons are wrapped up in a way that aids students in structuring their understanding and recollection of the lesson's core objectives (Dunlosky et al., 2013).

At the time, the ITIP model was both a practical and effective means for planning direct instruction and was readily embraced as this was the primary strategy used in classrooms. It streamlined practices in an efficient way that could be replicated day in and day out. Here lies the main disadvantage of ITIP. It was a one-size-fits-all approach centered on the teacher making all the decisions from an instructional standpoint at the expense of developing competent learners who can think.

Like many things in education, elements of ITIP still have value depending on how they are used. Closure is still critical to determine lesson effectiveness and serve as a catalyst for reflective growth. Exit tickets, when constructed well, represent a sound strategy to be implemented after a lesson. In simple terms, these are ungraded formative assessments that assess what students learned during the lesson. The data from them can be used to identify the following:

+ Level of mastery
+ Areas of difficulty
+ Opportunities to reteach
+ Gaps in learner understanding

First, suppose you are already using exit tickets or some other means of lesson closure. Take a minute to reflect on whether they are providing the type of substantive info outlined here or if they are merely making your lessons slightly longer. Consider if your closure elements might be tweaked to give you and your students greater value. As you approach future lessons, zero in on what these tasks tell you about student learning—individually and as a whole group. Are you seeing any patterns? How might you adjust your teaching to provide more focus where needed?

If exit tickets are new to you—what an opportunity! First, consider what feedback would be most helpful to you and your students. Then begin to craft what you want. Simply Google the term "exit tickets," and you will see several examples. Do not reinvent the wheel. Find one that fits your goals and modify it to make it yours. What lesson this week is a natural fit for an exit ticket? Choose one, develop your ticket, and try it with your class. Then, reflect on the information it provides—how does this align with your expectations around what you want your students to understand? What steps will you take to adjust your instruction? Remember, data is significant, but more important is what we do with the data.

A Teacher's Perspective

A few years back, I was a new teacher at Quest Academy, but not a new teacher in the classroom. When I started teaching at Quest Academy, I was jaded by the "system." I was burnt out and disillusioned like so many are when teaching in a traditional school setting. I was starting my 8th year and feeling like something needed to change. To my luck, Quest was the answer to my call. Before Quest, I was caught in the vicious cycle most of us know all too familiar with assigning work to my students, grading it on a 0-100% scale—"otherwise they would not do it"—giving a test only always to find myself asking, "Where in the process did I lose this student?"

To make matters worse, IF I DID NOT KNOW, HOW COULD THEY?

Feedback! This was the answer to my question. Finally, at Quest, I could answer these questions that haunted me for years! Here, I learned that simply giving points to students was not helping them learn or identify where they were in the learning process, nor was it helping me provide specific targeted interventions. We set out to create rubrics that allowed students to receive individual feedback and interventions at any point in the learning process.

Ask yourself how many times you have given a test worth 100 points, and a student who got a 70/100 knew exactly why and could share that with you, or how many times a student came back and WANTED to learn the concepts they had not yet mastered. In my case, very rarely, if ever, could a student tell me what concepts they had not yet mastered based on that extensive "70/100" written in red, circled in the corner of their test. Giving individual feedback throughout the learning process changed this for my students and me.

Our English Language Arts department set up a system in which students complete practices, which, by the way, are just that- a practice. A chance to learn and grow- NOT earn points. If students encounter an area in the practice in which they need additional instruction or reassurance, they meet with me during class, and we "conference." A conference is a quick meeting with the student to go over where they are in the learning process, using the learning targets I set for them to master along their learning progression. This allows us to work together to identify areas they may need additional reteaching or practice on.

Students have three practice lessons before taking a test, which assesses their level of understanding based on the horizontal criterion set on their rubrics. The wonderful thing about this is I have met with every student, YES, EVERY student, a minimum of three times before taking a test, so I no longer have to wonder "where I may have lost a student." Even better, the students know where they are in the learning process!

Feedback has become so ingrained in our school culture that students are open to learning and growing. They are open to asking for additional help when needed. Students at Quest understand that feedback is a learning tool. Transparency and clear communication create trust and encourage students to learn. The feedback is specific to them, NOT the whole class, giving meaning and importance to the message. It matters because you are taking the time to help them learn and grow. You are showing them you care about their learning. Earning points no longer matters because learning takes precedence over it.

All of this is achieved through constant individual feedback. Like many teachers, feedback allowed me to create the classroom I had always dreamed of, where learning is valued.

–Gigi Zavala, 9th Grade English Teacher

Bold Moves

Educators are called to embark on a bold adventure of transforming the learning experience into a deeply personalized and competency-based journey. This educational revolution starts by dismantling the traditional grading system, which often distorts the true purpose of education—learning and understanding—and replacing it with rubrics that reflect mastery and provide clear, actionable feedback. The narrative represents a change from teaching to the test to an emphasis on cultivating competencies students need to succeed in an unpredictable future. It proposes a shift in perspective, where students see errors not just as mistakes but as vital opportunities for growth and learning and where teachers act not as mere information deliverers but as coaches and mentors. This paradigm shift in education focuses on essential skills like communication, collaboration, creativity, and critical thinking and evolves them into competencies—a combination of knowledge, skills, behaviors, and attitudes.

In summary, the bold moves educators are encouraged to take involve a profound reassessment of teaching methods. It calls for focusing on authentic learning experiences over superficial point-gathering exercises, where learning is personalized, and assessments are meaningful. It underscores the need to view and treat students as unique learners, emphasizing that each student genuinely understands and masters learning instead of simply covering curriculum and content. Through such transformative approaches, educators can fulfill their true mission: to ignite a lifelong passion for learning and equip students with the skills and competencies required for success in a disruptive and dynamic world.

Great achievements often start with one bold action. This involves pausing to review the roadmap you've been using and setting a new direction, potentially taking us outside known areas or beyond the limits of your current work. The questions below will serve as your guide on this path to explore untapped possibilities.

1. How does the shift from a points-based system to a learning-oriented assessment reflect my daily teaching practice, and what steps am I taking to ensure students understand and apply this transformation approach?
2. How am I incorporating the concepts of personalized learning and competencies into the curriculum, and how does this change my approach to student assessment?
3. How can I ensure that my instructional strategies and assessment tools, like rubrics, are transparent and fair and promote mastery of competencies rather than just task completion?
4. What strategies am I employing, and why, to facilitate meaningful one-on-one interactions with students, develop a growth mindset, and treat errors as learning opportunities?
5. How do I use student feedback to adjust my teaching, and what mechanisms allow students to self-reflect on their learning journey and take ownership of their educational outcomes?

Share your progress on social media (Instagram, Twitter, LinkedIn, Facebook, TikTok) using the #**personalize** hashtag.

CHAPTER 5

Meeting Diverse Needs

In a community where everyday life barely slowed down, a school modeled innovation and understanding. In this school, there was a student named Emma whose journey through education had been influenced by challenges and triumphs. Emma, a bright and curious mind, often found herself lost in the traditional classroom setting, her unique learning needs fading into the background of a one-size-fits-all education system. However, this year was different, as the school had embraced a culture of differentiation aimed at supporting every student.

Emma's story of empowerment began when her new teacher, Mr. Jacobs, noticed her struggles and strengths in the first week of school. Unlike her previous experiences, Mr. Jacobs saw an opportunity to tailor the learning experience. He observed that Emma thrived on visual and hands-on learning, but traditional lectures and textbook assignments did not engage her as effectively. Recognizing this, Mr. Jacobs adapted his teaching methods, incorporating more visual aids, interactive projects, and group work that leveraged Emma's strengths and interests.

The turning point came during a unit on environmental science, a subject Emma was deeply passionate about but had struggled to excel in due to the conventional teaching methods used in the past. Mr. Jacobs introduced a project-based learning approach, where Emma could choose a topic related to environmental science that she was passionate about. Emma chose to explore renewable energy sources and their impact on the environment. She was given the freedom to present her research in a format that played to her strengths—creating a detailed model of a sustainable house powered by renewable energy, accompanied by a digital presentation.

Through this project, Emma's engagement and understanding soared. She collaborated with classmates, bringing her vision to life, and her presentation to the class showcased her deep understanding of the subject matter and her creativity and problem-solving skills. Mr. Jacobs provided structured choices, allowing Emma to work at her own pace offering feedback and support tailored to her learning preference. Emma felt seen and understood, her confidence grew, and her academic performance improved significantly.

Emma's success story spread throughout the school, serving as a reminder about the power of differentiation in education. It was not just about changing how subjects were taught but also how students were seen. Emma became an advocate for personalized learning, sharing her experiences and encouraging her peers and teachers to embrace the benefits of differentiation.

This story of empowerment reflects the profound impact that meeting individuals where they are through differentiation can have on a student's schooling. Emma's story is one of hope and a call to action for educators everywhere to see every student's unique potential and tailor their teaching to unlock that potential. In a world where education is the key to the future, differentiation stands as a powerful tool to ensure that every student, just like Emma, has the chance to succeed.

Real Differentiation

While distinct in their approaches, differentiated instruction and personalized learning share common goals and principles. It can indeed be viewed as a form of personalized learning, as both are centered on tailoring educational experiences for individual learners. Differentiation is fundamentally student-centric, focusing on adapting the content, process, and product based on student readiness, interests, and learning profiles. This approach acknowledges that students learn in different ways and at different paces, which is a cornerstone of personalized learning. When it comes to personalization, this concept is extended further by individualizing the learning experience even more, but differentiation serves as a vital component within a group setting.

There is one key difference. Differentiated instruction is more about what the teacher is doing by offering different options for learning the same core content. The teacher remains in control of the curriculum and guides the learning process, making informed decisions about the most effective way to teach each student or group of students. Creating an effective personalized environment hinges on the understanding and implementation of differentiation in three key areas: content, process, and product. This tailored approach ensures that all students, with their unique abilities, interests, and learning preferences, receive an education that caters specifically to them.

Differentiating Content

Differentiating content involves modifying what students learn or how they access the information. This can be achieved by using varied resources like books at different reading levels, videos, images, podcasts, and hands-on activities, which allow students to access material in a way that suits their learning preference. Connecting the content to topics that interest students can increase engagement and make learning more relevant. Providing choices in how they approach learning a topic, such as choosing between reading an article, watching a documentary, or conducting an experiment, is also effective. Tiered assignments that are designed to increase in complexity can ensure that all students start with fundamental concepts but can advance to more challenging material as they are ready.

Differentiating Process

The process of differentiation refers to how students make sense of the content. It involves flexible grouping, where students are rotated through different groups based on ability, interests, or preferences. This prevents pigeonholing and allows them to work with a variety of peers. Employing a mix of strategies, including hands-on activities, cooperative learning, and independent study, caters to different learning preferences. Learning centers or stations, which will be discussed later in this chapter, can be set up in the classroom to engage students with the material in various ways, each focusing on a different aspect of the topic or a different learning preference. Scaffolded learning, using support structures like graphic organizers or annotated examples, can guide students in their understanding.

Differentiating Product

Differentiating the product means varying the outputs or projects students create to demonstrate their understanding, as discussed in Chapter 3. This allows students to show what they know in a way that aligns with their strengths and interests. Allowing multiple formats for demonstrating knowledge, such as written reports, artistic projects, presentations, or videos, caters to different strengths. Providing rubrics with clear criteria that are flexible enough to accommodate various types of responses is crucial, as discussed in Chapter 4. Incorporating reflection opportunities helps students understand their strengths and areas for improvement. Peer feedback can provide different perspectives and ideas.

Differentiating content, process, and product is crucial for students in every classroom (Gregory & Chapman, 2007). Teachers can create a more inclusive and effective learning environment by implementing these strategies. Differentiation is not about creating separate lesson plans for each student but providing various avenues for students to access, engage with, and demonstrate their understanding of the content. This approach benefits students with different learning preferences and abilities and enriches the educational experience for all students.

Leveraging Data for Personalization

Teachers can adopt a multifaceted approach to data utilization to personalize learning in the classroom, leveraging both technological and non-technological means. Technology, such as learning management systems (LMS) and educational apps, offers analytics, providing insights into each student's engagement, comprehension, and progress (Ferguson, 2012). These tools can help teachers identify individual learning patterns, assess knowledge gaps, and customize educational content.

Without technology, formative assessments and observational data provide insights into individual learning needs, allowing for personalized feedback and support (Black & Wiliam, 1998). Examples include traditional methods like observations during class activities, common formative assessments, exit tickets, benchmark assessments, and one-on-one discussions, which offer invaluable data. These interactions allow educators to gauge students' understanding, motivations, and interests in real time, enabling the more effective adaptation of teaching strategies.

The first step involves gathering a wide range of data, including but not limited to standardized test scores, classroom assessments, observations, and student work samples. Technology can play a significant role here, with various educational software offering detailed reports on student performance across different competencies. Here are all the qualitative and quantitative data options that educators can use for personalized learning:

+ Common formative assessments (CFA's)
+ Routine standards-aligned benchmarks
+ Adaptive tools
+ Rubrics and proficiency scales
+ Exit tickets
+ Student work

By combining these data sources, teachers can develop a holistic view of each student's learning journey. For instance, technology can highlight areas where a student struggles, while personal interactions can provide context to these challenges, such as interests that could be leveraged to enhance understanding. This blend of quantitative and qualitative data equips teachers with the information to create personalized learning plans catering to their students' strengths, weaknesses, and interests.

Once data is collected, educators should segment it to analyze individual, group, and class performance. This involves looking for trends, such as common areas where students struggle or excel. Analysis tools, software, and artificial intelligence (AI) can help visualize these trends, making it easier to identify specific learning gaps. By comparing the data against learning standards or benchmarks, educators can pinpoint specific areas where students are not meeting expected outcomes. This step requires a deep understanding of the curriculum and the learning goals for each student.

With the learning gaps identified, educators can develop targeted interventions specific to individual students or groups. These interventions range from differentiated instruction and personalized learning plans to additional support outside the regular classroom setting. After implementing the targeted interventions, it is crucial to monitor progress closely. This involves collecting ongoing data to assess the effectiveness of the intervention. Adjustments should be made based on this data to ensure that the learning gaps are being closed. Educators should reflect on the effectiveness of their strategies and interventions. This reflection should consider the outcomes and the process of identifying and addressing learning gaps. Continuous professional development and collaboration with colleagues can enhance this reflection process.

Moreover, leveraging data for personalization also means setting achievable, tailored student goals, providing targeted feedback, and continuously adjusting learning pathways based on their progress. By embracing this data-enhanced approach, educators can improve the learning experience for every student, ensuring that they can reach their full potential. For educators seeking to deepen their understanding and application of these strategies, exploring current educational research and engaging in professional development opportunities focused on data-enhanced teaching can provide further insights and practical methods for implementing personalized learning in the classroom.

Tiered Interventions

Response to Intervention (RTI) is a process that supports learners at all levels. It represents a multi-tiered process to identify the behavior and learning needs of struggling students early on and then provide specific support through interventions. Below is a quick summary of the RTI components:

Tier 1—The teacher provides research-based instruction to the entire class, using extensive checks for understanding as a means of formative assessment. This data, along with that collected through routine benchmarking, is utilized to determine what supports are needed in Tier 2. Behavior screenings are also implemented.

Tier 2—Targeted supports are provided using the data collected from the Tier 1 interventions to provide small-group instruction focusing on specific learning and behavioral needs.

Tier 3 – At this level, the most at-risk students are provided individualized support, typically in a one-on-one setting.

There is a natural connection between RTI and personalization's essential elements and strategies. Earlier in this book, we shared that the driving premise of personalized learning is a focus on growth goals and interests to develop a greater sense of ownership of learning. Core elements include making instruction, pedagogy, and curriculum personal for students, which aids in alleviating many behavioral issues that arise. The use of data is also prevalent as a means to address individual weaknesses and build upon strengths. Successful personalization hinges on using high-agency strategies such as voice, choice, path, pace, and place throughout a lesson or unit of study.

Below, we have taken the traditional RTI pyramid of supports and added how personalized learning strategies could be implemented to ensure learners get what they need more effectively.

Personalized Learning Strategies for Effective RTI

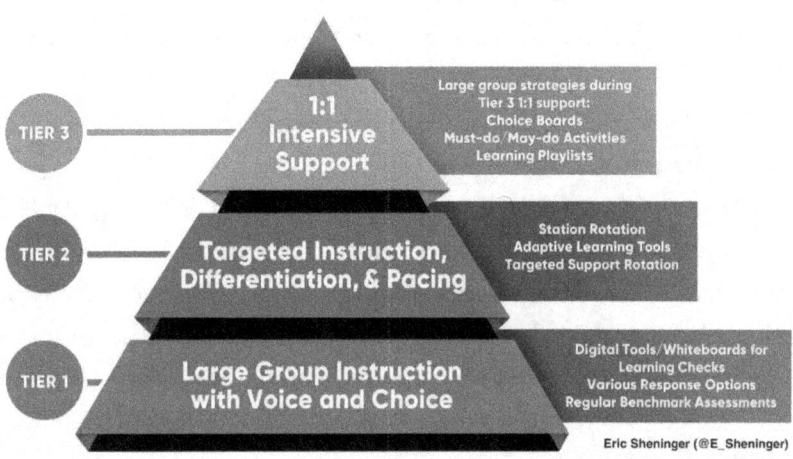

TIER 3 — **1:1 Intensive Support** — Large group strategies during Tier 3 1:1 support: Choice Boards Must-do/May-do Activities Learning Playlists

TIER 2 — **Targeted Instruction, Differentiation, & Pacing** — Station Rotation Adaptive Learning Tools Targeted Support Rotation

TIER 1 — **Large Group Instruction with Voice and Choice** — Digital Tools/Whiteboards for Learning Checks Various Response Options Regular Benchmark Assessments

Eric Sheninger (@E_Sheninger)

When designing interventions, keep in mind the following:

Tier 1 (Large group instruction with voice and choice)

The teacher makes learning more personal through student voice. Digital tools or individual whiteboards are used so that each child can respond to various checks for understanding, which can also screen students to determine Tier 2 supports. Choice is provided by allowing students different ways to respond to questions to amplify strengths. Benchmark assessments are provided at routine intervals to collect data for further screening. This can be done with or without technology.

Tier 2 (Targeted instruction, differentiation, and pacing via station rotation)

Data collected during Tier 1 is used to group students accordingly so the teacher can maximize available time to address learning gaps and behavior issues in a station rotation model, which will be described later in this chapter. While the tasks in the other rotations can vary, in an RTI model, an adaptive learning tool should be used in one of them to address weaknesses while allowing other students to move ahead at their own pace and path. If there is in-class support, a targeted support rotation could be established to provide greater assistance or screening.

Tier 3 (1:1 intensive support while the rest of the students work on differentiated choice activities or playlists)

The use of choice boards, must-do/may-do activities, and playlists, as discussed in Chapter 3, free up valuable time for the teacher to work with individual students. Data collected and the subsequent screening during Tiers 1 and 2 help identify the learners who need the most support. As the teacher works with one student, the rest of the class progresses through activities at their own pace along a path aligned with both ability and interests.

RTI has long been embraced as a strategy for students who either learn differently or have behavioral challenges that are stymying growth. Taking a more personalized approach, empowerment and learning ownership help alleviate many behavioral issues. Additionally, a more pragmatic approach is taken to collect, analyze, and use data to better screen and establish needed interventions. Consistent check-ins on behavioral patterns and learner progress help to ensure no student falls through the cracks, while personalization enhances and amplifies interventions. Hence, RTI and personalized learning are a dynamic duo.

Rotational Models

Helping learners is near and dear to our hearts. For me (Eric) the journey began in 2011 when we first introduced the flipped approach at New Milford High School (NJ), with resounding success. As I transitioned from the principalship to supporting districts and schools,

I learned that personalization was a robust collection of pedagogical strategies that could unleash students' potential.

Technology is a significant component, but not every activity has to incorporate some tool. The key is to find strategic ways to use it to improve learning. As we have covered in this book, there are many ways to personalize, but it is vital to have a firm understanding of the underlying premise of what you are trying to accomplish in terms of standards, concepts, and data and to maximize available class time to provide students with Tier 2 support. Enter station rotation.

With station rotation—or centers, as they are often referred to at the elementary level—the overarching goal is to use valuable class time more effectively. Following a short period of direct instruction with the entire class, the teacher breaks students into groups using data and the class engages in a series of activities during a set period. Each learner will visit all the stations, and a timer is used to let them know how long they have to engage in the activity. Typical stations include the following:

+ Targeted instruction or support
+ Collaborative experience
+ Personalization through the use of adaptive tools
+ Independent work

A teacher does not have to develop a set number of activities for this model. However, we most commonly see three or four. A modified two-station model could be used at the secondary level, where half the class works with the teacher while the other completes independent work using technology. We must get past the perception that this is just an "elementary" strategy. We have created a pedagogical framework to assist in setting up station rotation. You will see traditional elements of effective instruction at the front and back end. Using a valid data source for groupings is essential so the learners get the most out of the targeted instruction or support rotation. It is here where achievement gaps are closed, and students already at or beyond standard attainment can be pushed.

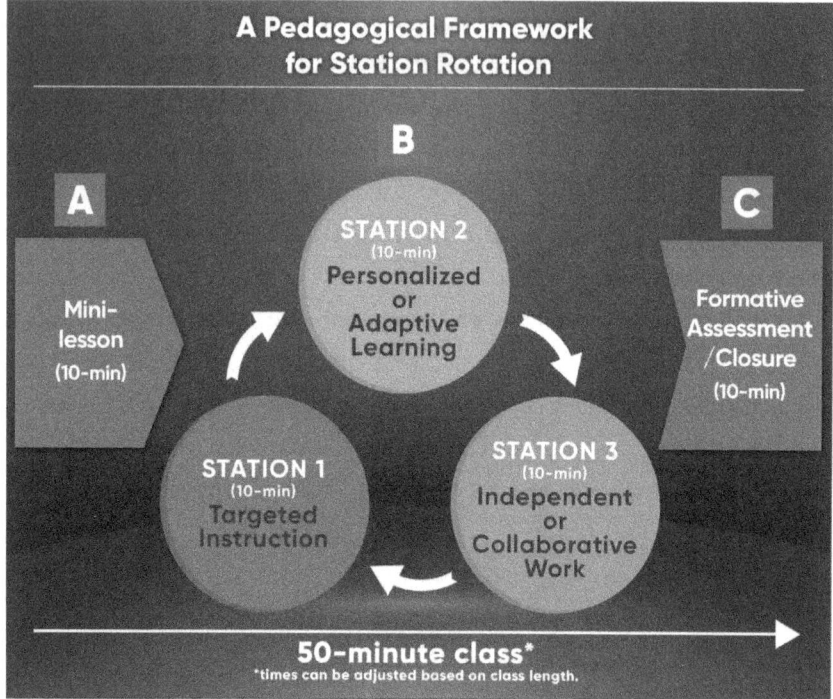

In addition to using data for groupings, a timer for pacing is also essential as it aids in self-regulation and time management. An important aspect is to build activities that promote collaboration. Here is where an interactive whiteboard (IWB) can be used to unlock its true potential. At a station with an IWB, students can work on collaborative projects or activities. The touch-sensitive display allows multiple students to interact with the board simultaneously, making it an excellent tool for brainstorming sessions, mind mapping, or group assignments. For example, students could collaboratively annotate a text, solve a complex math problem, or create a digital poster related to a unit of study. This encourages teamwork and the development of social skills, as students must communicate and negotiate roles and responsibilities.

The IWB can host self-paced learning activities where students interact with multimedia content, educational software, or web-based resources. This could include interactive reading activities, math games, or language learning apps. The IWB's large display and interactive features make it easier for students to navigate these activities and engage visually and tactilely. An IWB station can also be used for instant feedback and assessment. Students can complete quizzes or puzzles that instantly show results, allowing them to assess their understanding of the material. Teachers can utilize software that tracks progress over time, providing valuable data to inform instruction and offer personalized feedback to each student. This immediate feedback mechanism is vital for self-regulated learning, helping students identify areas of strength and those needing improvement.

When implementing station rotation consider the following:

+ Develop a template and share on screen and in LMS with context
+ Timer
+ Use data to group/regroup and target instruction
+ Integrate an adaptive learning tool
+ Keep rotations between 3-4
+ Use an exit ticket (three scaffolded questions/problems) at end of block for accountability

There is only one thing a teacher can control: how time is used when students are in class. While there is always a need for more time, it behooves us to think about existing opportunities to improve lesson effectiveness that lead to better outcomes. We know what some of you might be thinking: Station rotation sounds excellent in theory, but from a practical standpoint, it takes some time to plan when implementing it for the first time. We cannot argue with this point, but it is not accurate to say it cannot be done at all grade levels. Hence, we recommend a modified approach to how time is used, regardless of grade level. Here is the strategy:

+ Facilitate a mini-lesson that chunks the content.
+ Provide the whole class with an activity you would typically have planned.
+ While most of the class works on the assignment, pull small groups of students or individuals for targeted support.
+ Close the lesson.

Making the Most with the Time You've Got:
A Modified Approach to Personalized Learning

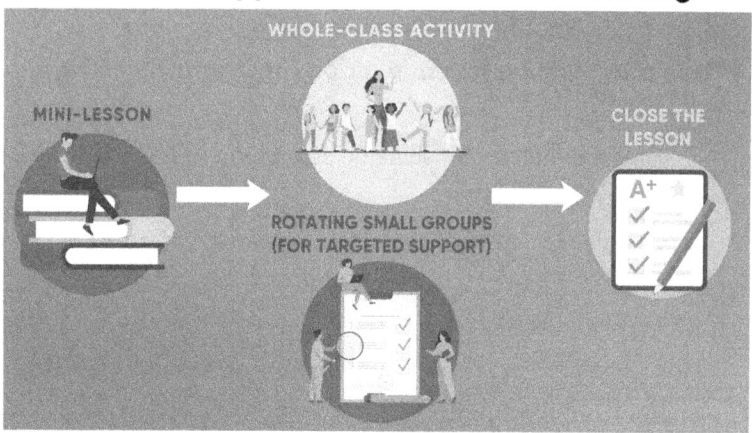

That is it in a nutshell. No extra time is spent planning, but support is provided within the period to those who need more help, especially at the secondary level, where the physical space might not cater to station rotation. Reflecting on how time is spent during class is essential if the goal is to improve learning and close achievement gaps.

Remember that there are many ways to set up this model, as you will see in the examples in Appendix 4. Overall efficacy relies on data being used to continuously group and regroup students, strategic use of adaptive learning tools, independent work that is rigorous and relevant, and the opportunity to collaborate actively. Again, there is only one thing educators can control: the time with students in the classroom. When used strategically, station rotation can differentiate while also building essential competencies such as time management and self-regulation. It is a win-win at any level.

Removing the Stigma of Intervention

In an ideal world, every student would have access to an education tailored to their unique needs and abilities. That is the goal we have set out to accomplish with this book. However, special education students often face more significant challenges that can impede their academic progress. One of the major hurdles they encounter is the stigma associated with intervention. This stigma affects students and perpetuates misconceptions about the purpose and effectiveness of interventions. Understanding the importance of removing the stigma surrounding intervention for special education students and developing practical ways to foster a more inclusive and supportive educational environment is vital.

REMOVING THE STIGMA OF INTERVENTIONS

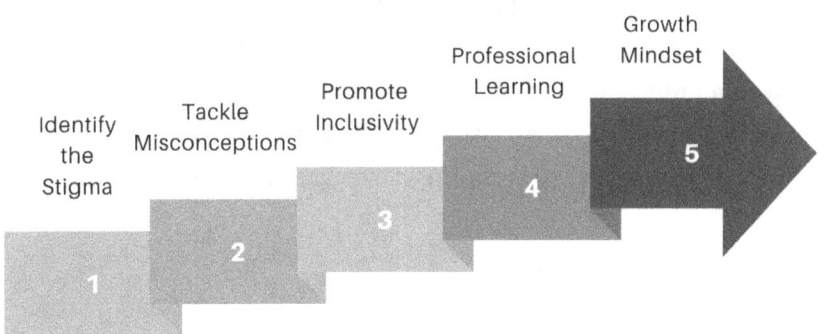

Understanding the Stigma

The stigma surrounding intervention for special education students stems from a combination of factors, including societal attitudes, lack of awareness, and the fear of being labeled. Many still hold outdated beliefs about special education, associating it with incompetence or intellectual limitations. This misconception can lead to a reluctance to embrace intervention strategies, even when proven beneficial.

Breaking Down Misconceptions

It is crucial to challenge and dispel common misconceptions about interventions to remove the stigma. Special education is a personalized method to address identified barriers to learning. Interventions do not reflect a student's intelligence; they are tools to help students overcome challenges and unlock their full potential. Educating parents, teachers, and the community about interventions' true nature and benefits is crucial in breaking down these barriers.

Promoting Inclusivity

Creating an inclusive environment is fundamental to removing the stigma associated with intervention. This involves acceptance and understanding in schools and communities. Emphasizing the diversity of learning preferences and celebrating the successes of all students can contribute to a more positive perception of interventions. Encouraging open communication and collaboration between teachers, parents, and students creates a support network that helps everyone involved understand the value of an intervention as a means to facilitate learning and growth.

Chasing Growth

Educators play a pivotal role in shaping students' experiences, and providing them with the necessary tools and knowledge is essential. Pursuing relevant opportunities to understand how to assist learners, intervention strategies, and the importance of personalized education can create a more inclusive classroom environment. When educators are well-equipped and confident in implementing interventions, it sends a powerful message that these strategies are a regular and integral part of the educational process.

Fostering a Growth Mindset

Encouraging a growth mindset among students is crucial to removing the stigma associated with interventions. Emphasizing that intelligence and abilities can be developed through dedication and diligent work rather than fixed traits helps students view interventions as valuable tools for improvement. Educators can help to build a culture that values effort and progress over innate talent to create a more positive and accepting atmosphere in which interventions are embraced rather than stigmatized.

Removing the stigma of intervention for special education students is a collective effort. We must recognize and embrace interventions to support their individual growth and success as a society. By working together, we can create an educational landscape that prioritizes the well-being and development of every student, regardless of their unique needs.

Effective Co-teaching Models

Effective co-teaching in classrooms leverages the strengths and expertise of each teacher to enhance instructional quality and provide the necessary learning support. According to Friend, Cook, Hurley-Chamberlain, and Shamberger (2010), effective co-teaching strategies involve shared planning, instruction, and assessment practices that accommodate a wide range of learning preferences and needs. Furthermore, Murawski and Swanson (2001) emphasize the significance of co-teaching for providing differentiated instruction, thereby improving academic outcomes for students with and without disabilities in inclusive settings. This collaborative model not only facilitates a more engaging and accessible learning environment but also models positive interpersonal skills and cooperative problem-solving for students.

The positive atmosphere and dynamic instructional strategies of effective co-teaching environments have significantly impacted student engagement and learning outcomes. Walsh and Jones (2019) found that co-taught classes often report higher student engagement and achievement levels, attributed to the varied instructional methods and increased individual support. Moreover, research by Scruggs, Mastropieri, and McDuffie (2007) supports the notion that students in co-taught settings experience more significant academic gains, particularly in inclusive classrooms where teachers employ various evidence-based practices. These findings underscore the importance of a well-coordinated, flexible approach to co-teaching, where ongoing communication and joint reflection on teaching practices are central to enhancing student learning and development.

Educators have a choice regarding the most effective co-teaching strategy to leverage. Here are six options to consider:

1. **One observe, one teach:** Before instruction, co-teachers collaboratively establish the specific observational data they intend to collect and concur on a data acquisition methodology. After the instruction, they collectively examine the gathered data. This collaborative process enhances the depth of observation regarding student engagement in the learning continuum.
2. **One assist, one teach:** In this co-teaching scenario, the instructional responsibilities are divided: one educator takes the lead

in facilitating the lesson, while the other discreetly moves among the students, offering help as required.

3. **Parallel teaching:** The teaching duo imparts identical content, partitioning the classroom into two cohorts for concurrent instruction that is differentiated based on ability and need.

4. **Alternative facilitation:** In this co-teaching arrangement, one educator leads the larger group's instruction while their counterpart focuses on a smaller group for targeted assistance.

5. **Duet teaching:** During team teaching sessions, the educators share the same classroom space and alternate roles in facilitating instruction to the entire class.

6. **Station rotation:** As discussed earlier in this chapter, educators instruct a designated group on specific content before delivering the same educational material to a different set of students. Additionally, they may set up separate station(s) designed for students to engage in solo or group tasks. In essence, targeted instruction happens simultaneously in two of the rotations.

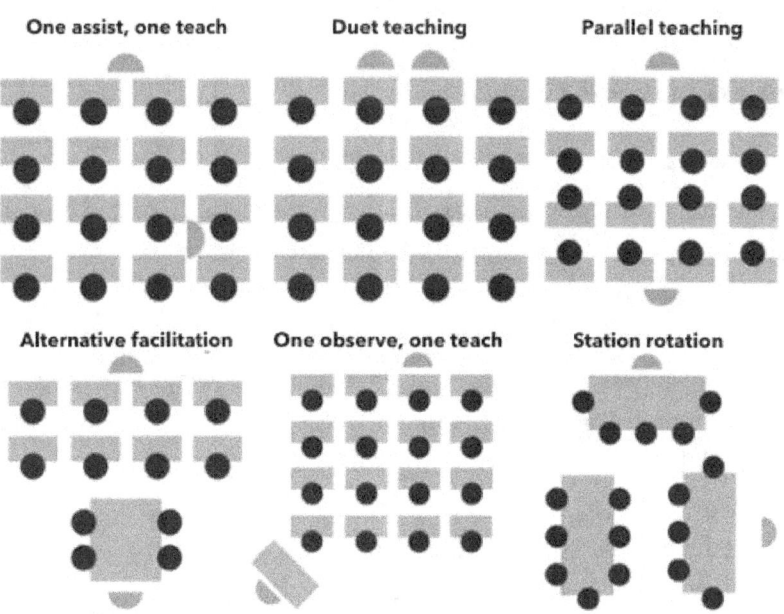

Effective co-teaching is a strategic pedagogical approach that inherently supports personalized learning by leveraging educators' strengths and expertise to support students. Grounded in research that underscores the value of educator collaboration, this method aligns with personalized learning by facilitating differentiated instruction, which is crucial for students with varying abilities and backgrounds. The co-teaching model is conducive to creating an environment ripe for personalized learning, as it allows for shared planning and assessment, enabling instruction that adapts to individual student preferences and learning goals.

Unlocking Potential with Artificial Intelligence

Artificial intelligence (AI) is a powerful tool that has the potential to revolutionize education by personalizing learning experiences for every student. Appendix 1 lists and describes powerful AI tools educators can use to plan, create rubrics, scaffold questions, and more. However, AI can be harnessed in much more powerful ways.

Adaptive Learning Paths

Learning paths provide a structured and personalized roadmap for a student's education, as discussed in Chapter 3. These paths guide students through their coursework, ensuring they receive content and challenges matching their skill levels and learning preferences. By tailoring the learning experience, students are more likely to remain engaged and motivated, which leads to better knowledge retention and a deeper understanding of the material. Learning paths also allow for self-paced learning, accommodating students who may need more time to grasp certain concepts and empowering those who progress quickly. Essentially, these paths provide a clear direction, sense of achievement, and help students reach their full potential.

AI's ability to analyze student data, such as their learning history and performance, allows for creating adaptive learning paths. These paths can be fine-tuned based on each student's strengths and weaknesses, ensuring they receive content that challenges them just enough to stimulate learning without causing frustration.

Customized Content

Customizing content in the classroom is essential because it acknowledges the diversity among students and recognizes that a one-size-fits-all approach to education is no longer practical. When we tailor content to align with students' interests, backgrounds, and preferred ways to learn, we create a more engaging and relevant learning experience. Customization can aid in deeper connections between the subject matter and students' real-life experiences, making it more relatable and meaningful. It also enhances student motivation and enthusiasm for learning, leading to better comprehension and retention of the material. Customized content empowers educators to meet students where they are, ensuring that every learner can thrive and reach their full potential, resulting in a more inclusive and effective educational environment.

One significant advantage of AI in education is its capacity to curate and deliver content that caters to individual preferences. With AI, teachers can select or create materials that align with students' interests, making the learning experience more engaging and relevant.

Providing Choice to Students

AI can significantly enhance the way teachers create choice boards by providing personalized and diverse learning options that cater to various student needs and learning preferences. By analyzing state standards and student performance data, AI can help educators design choice boards that integrate a variety of learning activities aligned with specific educational goals. For instance, AI can suggest multimedia resources, interactive tasks, and group projects tailored to different learning styles such as visual, auditory, and kinesthetic. AI can optimize these choice boards by continuously learning from student interactions and outcomes, ensuring that the activities not only meet educational standards but also engage students in meaningful and effective ways. This approach not only enriches the learning experience but also empowers students by offering them a menu of options that they can choose from based on their interests and learning preferences, ultimately creating a more inclusive and adaptable educational environment for students of all ages.

Real-time Feedback

Real-time feedback is critical to students because it offers immediate insights into their performance and understanding of the subject matter. Unlike traditional delayed feedback, which can lead to confusion and frustration, real-time feedback allows students to instantly correct mistakes, clarify doubts, and adjust their approach. This timely information helps students stay on track, maintain their motivation, and build a deeper understanding of the material as they progress. It also promotes a growth mindset by encouraging students to view mistakes as opportunities for improvement rather than failures. In essence, real-time feedback is a valuable tool in the learning process, as it enhances the quality of education and empowers students to become more self-directed and self-aware learners.

AI can provide students with instant feedback on their assignments and tests. This feature reduces the wait time for feedback and offers personalized suggestions for improvement, helping students understand and rectify their mistakes effectively.

Learning Preference Adaptation

Student learning preferences matter significantly because they recognize the individuality and uniqueness of each student. People have different cognitive styles, strengths, and ways of processing information. Educators can create a more inclusive and effective learning environment by acknowledging and accommodating these preferences. Tailoring teaching methods to match student preferences, whether visual, auditory, kinesthetic or combined, can enhance engagement and comprehension. When students are taught in ways that resonate with their learning preferences, they are more likely to be motivated, retain knowledge more effectively, and develop a more profound interest in the subject matter. Understanding and respecting these preferences not only maximizes the potential for academic success but also nurtures a positive and empowered learning experience for every student.

AI systems can identify a student's preferred preference, whether it is visual, auditory, or kinesthetic. This knowledge enables the system to deliver content in a format that best suits the individual, optimizing their learning experience.

Time Management Assistance

Time management is a crucial competency for students. It equips them for life in ways that extend far beyond the classroom. Learning to manage time effectively helps students meet deadlines, balance their academic and personal lives, and reduce stress. It encourages discipline, responsibility, and a sense of control over their education. Students who manage their time wisely tend to be more organized and efficient, allowing them to make the most of their learning experiences. Moreover, this skill prepares students for the demands of the professional world, where efficient time management is critical to success. Mastering time management is crucial for academic achievement and lays the foundation for a more balanced, productive, and fulfilling life. AI-powered tools can help learners manage their time efficiently by providing schedules and reminders tailored to their coursework, helping them stay on top of their assignments and study goals.

Predictive Analytics

Predictive analytics holds immense importance in improving student learning because it harnesses the power of data to foresee potential challenges and opportunities for each student. By analyzing historical performance, behavior, and engagement data, educators and institutions can identify students who may be at risk of falling behind or excel with additional challenges. This information allows for timely interventions, personalized support, and tailored educational resources, ensuring that no student is left behind and that each one can thrive in school. Predictive analytics empowers educators to make informed decisions, optimize the allocation of resources, and create a more proactive and student-centric learning environment, thus improving overall academic outcomes and enhancing the educational experience.

AI can predict students' future performance based on their achievements and behaviors. This information can be used to offer early intervention for students at risk of falling behind and ensure that they receive the necessary support to succeed.

Artificial intelligence holds the key to revolutionizing education by personalizing learning experiences. With adaptive learning paths, customized content, real-time feedback, learning preference adaptation, time management assistance, and predictive analytics, AI empowers educators to cater to each student's unique needs. As AI technology continues to evolve, it promises a future in which education is not just about transferring knowledge but also about individual growth and success. By embracing AI in education, we can build a more inclusive and effective learning environment for all students, unlocking their full potential.

Bold Moves

Personalization, grounded in differentiation, can effectively meet students' multifaceted needs. The story of a student named Emma and her teacher, Mr. Jacobs, exemplified this approach to education, which tailors teaching methods, materials, and assessments based on data and evidence, underscores the importance of flexibility to personalize in the modern classroom.

Educators looking to make bold moves toward implementing these strategies can begin by adopting a learner-centered mindset. This involves a deep commitment to understanding each student's unique background, interests, and abilities, much like Mr. Jacobs' dedication to recognizing Emma's preference for visual and hands-on learning activities. Teachers can conduct initial assessments to gather insights into their student's learning preferences and then design curriculum elements that offer various pathways to knowledge. They can also leverage multiple data sources to make the most effective pedagogical decisions to help all learners succeed. Incorporating technology, such as interactive whiteboards, adaptive learning software, and artificial intelligence (AI), can further personalize the learning experience, allowing students to engage with material at their own pace and in their preferred learning modality.

Another bold step involves classrooms that value diversity in learning and encourage risk-taking and experimentation. Educators must be open to restructuring traditional classroom layouts, schedules, and teaching methods to facilitate small group work, peer tutoring, and project-based learning initiatives that reflect real-world problems and interests. Professional learning opportunities focused on differentiation, rotational models, use of data, and co-teaching can equip teachers with the strategies and confidence needed to implement these changes effectively.

By creating an inclusive and dynamic learning environment, educators can ensure that each student, like Emma, feels valued, understood, and empowered to reach their full potential. The questions below will assist you in making bold moves that result in this shift.

1. Reflecting on my current practices, how is data being utilized effectively to group, regroup, target instruction, and differentiate? Where is there an opportunity for growth?
2. How am I leveraging technology to support my classroom's diverse learning needs and preferences? Are there tools or resources I could explore to enhance personalized learning experiences for my students?
3. In what ways am I cultivating an inclusive classroom environment that empowers all students to feel valued, respected, and capable of achieving their full potential? How can I better implement intervention and co-teaching strategies?
4. Explain how you could redesign your current Tier 2 and Tier 3 interventions to incorporate more personalized learning elements like station rotations, playlists, and student choice activities. How would this approach benefit struggling learners and advanced students within the same intervention group?
5. Identify a specific learning objective or unit in your current curriculum that could benefit from an adaptive learning path. How could you leverage AI tools to design a personalized learning pathway for your students considering their strengths, weaknesses, and learning preferences? What data points would be most valuable to consider when creating these pathways?

Share your progress on social media (Instagram, Twitter, LinkedIn, Facebook, TikTok) using the **#personalize** hashtag.

CHAPTER 6

Relationships Above All Else

Recognized for his unconventional methods, Mr. Anderson believed sincerely in the power of establishing positive relationships with his students. He knew that beyond the curriculum lay the true essence of teaching—connecting with each student to ignite their potential. It was not only about delivering lessons, but also understanding their hopes, fears, and challenges. This belief set the stage for a transformative year for Mr. Anderson and his students.

One student in particular, Leo, struggled with engagement and motivation. Past teachers had found him demanding, often sidelining him as uninterested. However, Mr. Anderson saw a spark in Leo that others had missed. By getting to know him, Mr. Anderson discovered Leo's passion for art and used this to connect lessons with what Leo loved. This personalized approach broke down barriers, and slowly, Leo began to participate, his confidence blooming with each class. Mr. Anderson's relationship with Leo transformed his academic performance and self-belief.

Mr. Anderson's approach rippled through his classroom, creating a culture of trust and respect. Students were no longer just attendees but active participants in a shared learning journey. This environment led to a sense of belonging and encouraged students to take risks, ask questions, and express themselves freely, knowing they were supported. By the year's end, Mr. Anderson's class was academically successful and emotionally resilient. The transformation underscored a profound lesson: the foundation of effective teaching lies in the genuine connections teachers forge with their students.

Building and Strengthening the Foundation

In the pursuit to create a nurturing and effective personalized environment, teachers must genuinely know their learners. This involves understanding their academic abilities, learning preferences, personal interests, cultural backgrounds, and emotional needs. Here are specific strategies teachers can employ to achieve this:

Conduct Interest Surveys and Inventories: At the beginning of the school year or semester, teachers can use surveys or questionnaires to gather information about students' hobbies, interests, strengths, and even concerns about the subject or school. This helps the teacher tailor instruction to students' interests and shows that the teacher values the students' input.

One-on-One Meetings: Scheduling brief, regular check-ins with students can provide insight into their progress and challenges. These meetings can be informal chats where students feel comfortable sharing personal insights, aspirations, and struggles.

Learning Profiles: Teachers can develop learning profiles for each student based on observation, assessment data, and students' self-reports. These profiles help differentiate instruction and provide appropriate challenges for each learner.

Cultural Competence: Teachers need to be aware of and sensitive to the various cultural backgrounds represented in their classroom. This might involve professional development in cultural competence, learning about students' cultural contexts, and incorporating culturally responsive teaching practices.

Classroom Community Building: Teachers can facilitate activities that promote a sense of community within the classroom, such as collaborative projects, class discussions, and group problem-solving activities. These activities build relationships and allow teachers to observe how students work with others and understand their social dynamics.

Home-School Connections: Reaching out to families through parent-teacher conferences, newsletters, and events helps teachers learn more about their students' lives outside of school. This broader perspective can inform approaches to support the child's learning.

Reflective Practices: Teachers can keep reflective journals about their daily interactions and observations of students. Reflective practice allows for continuous adaptation and improvement of strategies.

By incorporating these strategies, teachers not only enhance their understanding of each student as an individual but also create a learning atmosphere that is respectful, responsive, and conducive to each student's growth. This relationship-driven approach improves student engagement, motivation, and academic success.

A Framework for Relational Learning

In the ever-evolving personalized landscape, relational learning emerges as a fundamental component. At its core, it underscores the importance of building connections between concepts, leading to a deep and interconnected understanding of subjects. However, the significance of relational learning extends beyond the academic realm, as it emphasizes cultivating trust-centered relationships among students and educators.

Relational learning matters because it addresses the shortcomings of traditional memorization-based approaches, something we have emphasized as a critical tenet of personalization. Rather than viewing topics in isolation, this method encourages students to explore the interconnectedness of ideas. Students develop critical thinking skills essential for success in academic and real-world scenarios by recognizing and understanding relationships between concepts. Drawing connections between seemingly disparate pieces of information enhances comprehension and retention, providing a foundation for lifelong learning.

Relational learning, which emphasizes the importance of social connections and emotional engagement in the educational process, is foundational for student success. Research has shown that when students feel a strong relational connection to their teachers and peers, they are more likely to engage deeply with content and persist in the face of challenges (Pianta, 1999; Roorda et al., 2011). Moreover, schools prioritizing relational learning often see improvements in student attendance, academic achievement, and reduced disruptive behavior, as these environments meet students' developmental needs for belonging and significance (Osterman, 2000; Cornelius-White, 2007).

Beyond its cognitive benefits, relational learning contributes to creating a positive and collaborative classroom environment. Building relationships among students and between students and teachers is a crucial aspect of this approach. When students feel a sense of connection and trust, they are more likely to engage in meaningful discussions, share ideas, and collaborate on projects. These interpersonal skills are essential for academic success and mirror the professional world's collaborative nature, where effective teamwork is highly valued.

To implement relational learning effectively, educators must prioritize establishing positive relationships within the classroom. Creating a supportive and inclusive environment where students feel comfortable expressing their thoughts and opinions is essential, which is why the learner's voice matters. Educators can achieve this through open communication, actively listening to students, and demonstrating genuine interest in their journeys. Building relationships also involves recognizing and appreciating the backgrounds, experiences, and learning preferences present in the classroom, which translates into an inclusive atmosphere that celebrates uniqueness.

In addition to building relationships, successful implementation of relational learning requires thoughtful curriculum design and instructional strategies. Incorporating real-world examples, case studies, and interactive activities highlighting the relationships between concepts can make learning more engaging and relevant for students. Technology can also play a crucial role by providing multimedia resources to explore and understand interconnected ideas.

Assessment methods should align with the principles of relational learning, emphasizing understanding and competency development over rote memorization. Assessments can include tasks that require students to demonstrate their ability to identify and articulate relationships between concepts. This change in assessment encourages students to develop analytical skills and reinforces the value of relational learning in their schooling.

This iteration of the Relevant Thinking Framework focuses on the importance of relationships. As discussed in Chapter 2, the framework can support and enhance instruction and pedagogy by integrating various pivotal competencies for personalized learning. It consists of four main quadrants, A, B, C, and D, each representing a different combination of skills and educational focus. These quadrants are enveloped by a circular band highlighting relationships' importance in the learning process.

Each quadrant combines two axes: one for the level of cognitive demand (from low to high) and one for the application level to real-world scenarios (from low to high). The cognitive skills axis is about thinking, and the application axis is about doing, and together, they provide a comprehensive approach to learning.

Quadrant A (Acquisition) is at the lower end of both axes, signifying fundamental understanding and knowledge acquisition. Here, students absorb information and learn basic skills, which form the foundation for more advanced learning. This level focuses on traditional teaching methods such as lectures, rote memorization, and basic exercises.

Quadrant B (Application) still involves lower-level cognitive skills but with a higher level of real-world relevance. Students begin to apply what they have learned to practical situations. This can include activities like case studies, simple experiments, and hands-on tasks that connect learning to the real world.

Quadrant C (Assimilation) requires higher-level cognitive skills but needs to be more focused on direct real-world application. Students analyze, compare, and synthesize information in this quadrant, developing their critical thinking and problem-solving capacity within theoretical or hypothetical contexts.

Quadrant D (Adaptation) represents the highest level of cognitive demand and real-world application. Students are expected to extend their learning beyond the classroom, tackling complex problems, innovating, and making decisions based on in-depth understanding and analysis of real-world challenges. This involves project-based learning, research initiatives, and other forms of inquiry that promote independence and creativity.

Encircling these quadrants is a band divided into three overlapping segments: Emotional, Social and Interpersonal, and Cognitive skills, the latter of which is explained above. Emotional skills encompass the ability to recognize and manage one's emotions and those of others. Social and interpersonal skills refer to the abilities needed to interact effectively with others, including communication, collaboration, and conflict resolution.

The emphasis on relationships in this framework iteration highlights the integral role that connections between students, educators, and the community play in the educational process. Firm, supportive relationships enhance engagement and learning outcomes. It emphasizes that education is about content and skills, community-building, and connecting with others. This is where the emotional and social aspects come into play, enabling students to develop empathy, respect, and a sense of social responsibility.

Through this framework, educators are encouraged to craft a learning environment that challenges students intellectually and supports their emotional and social development. It acknowledges that learning is most effective when it is relational, when students feel seen and valued, and when they can connect their learning to their lives and those of others around them.

Relational learning is a cornerstone of personalization, promoting cognitive development and establishing meaningful relationships within the classroom. The successful implementation of this approach involves a dual focus on curriculum design and the intentional cultivation of positive relationships. By prioritizing relational learning and building connections within the classroom, educators can create an environment that nurtures holistic understanding, critical thinking, and interpersonal skills essential for success in both academic and real-world settings.

Daily Routines

The emotions of students are all over the place. These stem from a variety of factors, including isolation, excessive time on social media, watching parents struggle financially, and pressure to get good grades. Uncontrolled or unchecked emotions lead to negative effects on learning. It is challenging to learn and concentrate if the mind is pulled in numerous directions. This is not an issue that only impacts kids. Efforts need to be made, and an array of supports should be offered to ensure the well-being of staff members also, especially those who are in direct contact with students daily.

Let us start with students. For Social Emotional Learning (SEL) to be more than a buzzword or fad, it should be embedded across an array of practices. If we want students to open up to us, we need to be intentional about earning their trust. In addition, we must embrace strategies to identify, monitor, and support kids dealing with social and emotional issues impacting their learning and their peers.

Venola Mason (2021) shares one such relationship-building tool called *Pause & React*:

"I have noticed in classrooms across the country that educators use the first days and weeks of school to build relationships and connect with students. However, as the school year progresses and more attention is paid to academic content, less emphasis is placed on maintaining these critical relationships. Often, students who experience trauma or other difficulties are overlooked until their situation becomes very severe, leaving teachers unsure of how to turn things around. What I arrived at to help address this need is a practical and straightforward resource for approaching relationship-building—a tool I call PAUSE & REACT. It is meant to be simple—not another thing to add to a teacher's plate, but an intuitive and structured way to leverage and strengthen relationships with students. (pg. 40)."

Pause & React

A tool for cultivating strong teacher–student relationships

 Pay Attention

Look for changes in disposition, behavior, or habits.

 Ask Questions

Uncover the specifics behind why this change is occurring.
(I noticed...and I'm wondering...?)

Use Your Expertise

Determine if other adults should be involved.
(school psychologist, principal, parent, etc.)

Show Genuine Interest

Show the student that their wellbeing is important to you.

Evaluate The Circumstances

Review all of the evidence to determine a plan of action.

Reach Out

Create a team of support for the student.
(teachers, coaches, counselors, etc.)

Extend A Helping Hand

Provide direct support to the student.

Assume The Best

Presume positive intentions.

Create Opportunites

Connect the student to opportunities within and outside of the classroom.

Tap Into Their Greatness

Set the student up for success by building on their interests and strengths.

Relationship building and repairing relationships should be an embedded component of a personalized learning culture. Here are some practical strategies that can be easily implemented daily and across the curriculum to accomplish this:

Daily meeting: Many educators have heard of the Morning Meeting, where students engage in various SEL activities before starting content-related lessons. While this is a great strategy, it should rotate throughout the day so it does not occur during the same time or period each day.

Lesson planning/activities: While daily meetings are a great start, SEL should be emphasized throughout the curriculum. Sound pedagogy can be the most proactive approach available to meeting students' social and emotional needs daily. Every personalized model can include an opportunity for socialization or conferencing with the teacher.

Digital surveys – During a coaching visit with the Juab School District in Utah, we saw a teacher begin the day with a digital survey that included the following: How are you feeling today? Why do you feel that way? Do you need to conference with the teacher? While the rest of the class worked on a choice STEAM activity, the teacher conferenced with those kids who needed non-academic support.

Family engagement: SEL should never be the sole responsibility of teachers. Consistent programs and outreach to families highlighting strategies and resources that can be used at home to identify and support students are critical.

If we do not care for all of our people—students, teachers, support staff, and administrators—our education system will never function to its full potential.

Building Stakeholder Connections

Engaging with parents, families, and the broader community allows educators to gain distinct perspectives and insights, which are invaluable in tailoring educational experiences to fit each student uniquely. This collaborative approach ensures that learning is aligned with academic standards and students' personal interests and life goals, making education more relevant and impactful. Stakeholder involvement supports shared responsibility for student success, providing a network of assistance that extends beyond the classroom. By actively involving stakeholders in the learning process, educators can leverage a broader range of resources, experiences, and expertise, enriching the personalized learning experience and promoting student engagement, motivation, and achievement.

Educators can employ a multifaceted approach centered around communication, engagement, and collaboration to forge powerful connections with stakeholders—students, parents, colleagues, and the broader community. It all begins with communication.

It is hard to deny how important communication is for any educator. In many cases, it will make or break their success. You will not find an effective educator who is also not an effective communicator (Sheninger, 2019). Moving to a personalized teaching and learning culture requires that we communicate openly and often with all stakeholders, implementing intentional communication strategies to build support for the work.

When crafting a strategy to help your stakeholders understand the importance of personalized approaches to teaching and learning, it is always critical to think about the following before preparing any message or interaction:

+ Why is this message important to communicate, and when should it be communicated?
+ How will I convey the information?
+ What will tell me if I have been successful?

The above questions provide an excellent foundation for effective communication. Here are some ideas for harnessing these questions to ensure that your communication has an impact and, in the process, builds powerful relationships with and beyond your community.

Get the Message Across

Although *developing* the message is extremely important, *how it is delivered* is equally important. By leveraging a situational approach, educators can determine the best strategy with the most impact. Sometimes, this might be an email, while other times, it can be a phone call, handwritten note, or social media post that includes text, images, videos, or links. Different situations call for different approaches. The bottom line is that getting the message across requires flexibility and an openness to various means at your disposal.

Knowing your audience is also about accepting that someone other than you might be the best person to communicate the message. Former Duke University basketball coach Mike Krzyzewski shared, "Recognize that yours is not the only voice your team wants or needs to hear and be unselfish with your leadership. Allowing others to lead and using their voices shows you are a stronger leader. Their voices can help you increase your team's attention-span window and often convey a message that resonates in a way that could never have come from the leader." (Geier, 2019).

Understand Your Audience

Just because you prefer a specific means of communication or technique does not infer that your stakeholders do as well. The same can be true about the information that you feel is valuable to convey. Just as teachers differentiate for a variety of learning preferences in the classroom, educators need to differentiate their communication efforts if we want true stakeholder partnerships between home, school, and the greater community (Sheninger, 2019). Communication and community relations are among the nine most essential skills for educators to master (Hoyle, et al. 1998).

Your audience is comprised of different demographics and age groups. In the digital age, we must embrace a multifaceted approach that meets stakeholders where they are while engaging them in two-way communication. Popular tools such as Snapchat and TikTok are just as valuable, if not more so, than Twitter, Facebook, and Instagram. While social media should play a significant role in engaging your audience and getting the message across, technology is not and never will be the only way to communicate with stakeholders. Whether communicating via technology or more traditional means, remember: stories that pull at different emotions are always powerful ways to connect with your audience.

Connect to Personalization

Whether you are disseminating information, providing feedback, or educating your stakeholders, there must be a compelling *why*, a clear *how*, and a definitive *what* in connection with personalization that leads to the message resonating with your audience. Effective educators address concerns and proudly share all that is being done to help learners succeed. While exceptions exist, you can rarely go wrong when you frame communications around learning, the core purpose of education.

Here are specific strategies that can help you show stakeholders the value and power of personalization:

1. Elevate everyday excellence in your classroom, school, or district by employing a communication strategy that integrates classic methods (newsletters, emails, phone calls, in-person discussions) with modern digital tools (social media platforms). Be sure to differentiate with text, images, and videos that capture student work and outcomes. Ensure that your social media profiles are current, with accurate website links and profile details. Create or use a hashtag (#) unique to your school or district to amplify messaging and curate the collective

work in a way that is easy to access. Additionally, it is crucial to educate parents and community members about these digital platforms and their use to increase involvement.

2. Nurture trust by embracing openness. The advantages of this are many, leading to outcomes including garnering support from families. By maintaining transparent and regular communication, educators can share insights about a student's academic progress, behavioral patterns, and social interactions, enabling parents to understand and support their child's personalized learning journey effectively. This dialogue helps in aligning the educational goals and strategies between home and school, ensuring that both educators and parents work collaboratively towards the student's development.

3. Concentrate on aspects indicative of a flourishing personalized culture, such as cutting-edge learning techniques, student successes, staff achievements, readiness for college or careers, collaborative initiatives, distinctive traditions, and extracurricular programs.

4. Embrace collective storytelling within your school community by sharing how you effectively personalize and encourage various groups—grade level teams, academic departments, student clubs, and parent organizations—to share their narratives through their social media channels.

5. Acknowledge staff and student efforts regularly. This increases motivation and appreciation, contributing to a positive educational atmosphere. If you are a leader, consider establishing a monthly roundup template to highlight and celebrate the exceptional work happening throughout the school.

Impactful communication is a catalyst for meaningful change. In the words of Dr. Michelle Mazur, "When you start communicating to change people, you leave a legacy. You profit from your impact, not in spite of it. Mazur, 2019.) Remember that leadership is about action, not title, position, or power. All educators can leverage effective communication strategies to show the value of personalization while forging priceless relationships in the

> Remember that leadership is about action, not title, position, or power.

process. This sets the stage for collaborative approaches to build powerful relationships and support for personalization further.

Offering opportunities for stakeholder engagement, such as parent-teacher meetings and community events, invites active participation in the educational process. Listening attentively to stakeholder feedback through surveys and forums and acting on this feedback develops a culture of trust and respect. Building collaborative partnerships with parents, local businesses, and community organizations can significantly enhance the learning experience by providing valuable resources and real-world connections. Making personal connections by recognizing individual achievements and showing genuine interest deepens relationships. Transparency in educational goals and decisions builds trust while celebrating community successes reinforces a sense of shared achievement and value.

Continuous professional development focused on enhancing stakeholder engagement further equips educators with innovative strategies to strengthen these relationships. By embracing these approaches, educators can create a supportive, inclusive, and collaborative educational environment that benefits all stakeholders and enhances the learning experience for students.

Bold Moves

Personalization hinges on understanding students' unique needs, interests, and backgrounds. Educators can conduct interest surveys and one-on-one meetings, develop learning profiles, and build a classroom community to create a responsive educational environment. Relational learning is a critical component of this process, because it can build strong connections among students and educators to facilitate a deeper understanding of subjects and improve engagement, motivation, and academic success. By prioritizing these approaches, educators can shift towards more personalized and effective teaching practices, advancing a more engaging, supportive, and inclusive learning atmosphere.

We encourage educators to adopt innovative practices that go beyond traditional educational models. They can create a more dynamic and engaging learning environment by implementing personalized learning plans, utilizing technology for adaptive learning, and encouraging collaborative projects that reflect real-world problems. Furthermore, an atmosphere of trust and open communication enables students to take risks and explore their interests deeply, enhancing their critical thinking and problem-solving skills.

Professional learning helps educators stay abreast of the latest educational research and technologies, ensuring that their teaching methods remain relevant and effective in preparing students for the future. Through these bold moves, educators can revolutionize the learning experience, making it more comprehensive, engaging, and aligned with the student growth goals. The questions below will help get you there.

1. How do I actively learn about my students' backgrounds, interests, and learning preferences to tailor my teaching approach? Where is there an opportunity to grow?
2. How do I cultivate a classroom environment that encourages relational learning and builds strong connections among students and between students and myself?
3. What strategies do I use to integrate real-world examples and interactive activities highlighting the relationships between concepts in my teaching?

4. Reflecting on my current practices, what steps can I take to embrace further and implement personalized and relational learning approaches in my classroom?

5. How can educators effectively communicate the benefits and methodologies of personalized learning approaches to stakeholders (parents, administrators, and community members) to gain their support and involvement?

Share your progress on social media (Instagram, Twitter, LinkedIn, Facebook, TikTok) using the **#personalize** hashtag.

CHAPTER 7

Embrace the Journey

Transitioning from traditional teaching methods to personalized approaches presents educators with many challenges, but also opportunities for personal and professional growth. Central to this transition is the need for self-reflection, which reignites the passion for teaching and provides the strength to explore proven strategies. There is no prescribed route to personalizing education; it demands a fusion of established methodologies and innovative concepts.

As this book ends, we invite you to start your journey where traditional practices merge seamlessly with novel approaches. Embracing this odyssey requires acknowledging that it encompasses more than just reaching an endpoint—it is about embracing the inherent transformative power of education itself. Each progressive step taken along this path will bring you closer to unlocking the full potential of every student and cultivating an environment of inclusivity and empowerment. Remember, there is not one right way to personalize education; it is your journey geared to helping all learners succeed.

Fall in Love with Teaching Again

Ms. Slay made her way to her classroom, burdened by the weight of routine tasks awaiting her. She felt uninspired by the required standardized curriculum, frustrated by the lack of autonomy and feeling micromanaged, with little control over her teaching methods. A stack of papers called for her attention, requiring hours spent correcting and inputting grades rather than engaging deeply with lesson planning or student support. The repetitive tasks and unengaging lessons she presented to her students had dimmed her enthusiasm for teaching.

Looking around the room at her disengaged students, Ms. Slay felt a shared sense of disconnect. However, a glimmer of hope emerged—a desire to break free from routine and move towards personalized learning. She embarked on this journey with determination, empowering herself to design learning experiences that created an environment in which students could be excited to learn, actively collaborating, and choosing learning activities and methods that fit their personal learning preferences.

Ms. Slay took time to develop meaningful connections with her students and allowed for student agency. Through individualized feedback and a culture that emphasized a growth mindset, she created a classroom where students felt valued and motivated.

As weeks passed, Ms. Slay witnessed her students transform as learners. Freed from routine and cookie-cutter instruction, she focused on teaching differentiated small group lessons, facilitating discussions that led to deep understanding, creating choice activities to give students ownership of their learning, and providing collaborative projects that increase communication and problem-solving skills in her students.

Ultimately, Ms. Slay's commitment to personalized learning reignited her passion and enriched her students' educational experiences. Adding relevant and exciting content made students more deeply engaged, attendance increased, and everyone was happier. Ms. Slay fell in love with her job again.

The current educational landscape often feels suffocating, with teachers overwhelmed by endless grading, administrative tasks, and a rigid one-size-fits-all approach to instruction. The lack of personalization hampers student engagement and contributes to teacher burnout and disillusionment.

In a system filled with repetitive tasks and standardized curricula, many teachers find themselves at a crossroads, questioning their impact and longing for change. Do you yearn to reignite the passion you once had for your profession? Are you drained, exhausted, and seeking a renewed sense of purpose? These questions resonate deeply with educators navigating the challenges of modern teaching. Amidst the obstacles lies a beacon of hope: personalized learning. By shifting towards a more tailored approach to education, teachers can reclaim their passion and redefine their purpose in the classroom. Personalized learning empowers educators to create dynamic, student-centered experiences.

Remember Your Why

In education, one truth remains constant: our primary responsibility is to meet the needs of our students. Regardless of the age group or setting, this commitment to personalization is not just a best practice but the essence of what we do. In the face of challenges, it is vital to draw strength from the mantra: "They never said it was easy; they just said it was worth it."

> In education, one truth remains constant: our primary responsibility is to meet the needs of our students.

During moments of weariness or frustration, it is imperative to reconnect with your "why." As you finish this book, reflect on when you decided to pursue this noble profession and identify what intrinsic motivations were behind it to reignite your passion and sense of purpose. By articulating your thoughts and emotions on paper, you will find solace in reaffirming your commitment to the betterment of our students. Displaying these reflections prominently reminds us of our unwavering dedication to prioritize their growth above all else.

Engaging in this reflective exercise will often lead you to realize that your frustrations stem not from the students themselves but from systemic or procedural challenges that undermine your sense of fulfillment. It underscores the importance of advocating for meaningful and purposeful practices within the educational landscape.

Research on happiness at Stanford University offers valuable insights into the transformative power of aligning our careers with our passions. These findings serve as a reminder of the profound impact of pursuing our true calling, resonating deeply with our pursuit toward happiness and fulfillment in teaching (Brooks & Winfrey, 2023). It is critical to find purpose and meaning in one's work. When individuals align their careers with their values and passions, they experience greater fulfillment and satisfaction. Engaging in work that allows for meaningful contributions to others' well-being can significantly enhance happiness. This could involve professions that involve caregiving, teaching, volunteering, or any role that involves helping others.

Social connections and relationships are crucial in stimulating happiness. Cultivating solid bonds with colleagues, friends, and family can positively impact overall well-being. A key finding in this study is that having a sense of autonomy and control over one's work is crucial for happiness. Jobs that provide opportunities for creativity, decision-making, and personal growth are often associated with higher levels of job satisfaction. This is the opportunity we give our students when we shift to personalization.

In addition to reflecting on Brooks' research, consider implementing practical strategies to reconnect with your "why" in education:

1. **Regular Reflection Sessions:** Set aside dedicated time in your schedule for reflection. This will allow you to revisit your initial motivations for entering the teaching profession and assess how they align with your current practices and experiences.

2. **Seek Mentorship and Peer Support:** Connect with mentors or colleagues who can offer guidance and support during challenging times. Sharing experiences and gaining fresh perspectives can help you maintain perspective and rediscover your passion for teaching.

3. **Professional Learning Opportunities:** Engage in activities focusing on personal growth and aligning your values. Attend workshops, seminars, or conferences that address topics relevant to your interests and aspirations as an educator.

4. **Cultivate a Culture of Appreciation:** Foster a culture of appreciation within your educational institution by recognizing and celebrating the contributions of educators. Feeling valued and appreciated can reinforce your sense of purpose and commitment to your students.

5. **Explore Creative Teaching Approaches:** Experiment with innovative teaching approaches or projects that align with your interests and values. Incorporating creativity into your teaching practice can reignite your enthusiasm and sense of fulfillment.

By implementing these practical strategies, you can proactively reconnect with your "why," sustaining your passion and motivation as an educator. Remember, your dedication to the betterment of students is the driving force behind your noble profession.

The Best Way is Your Way

In education, there is no universal formula for success. Instead, the key lies in embracing the uniqueness of each educator, each classroom, each school, and each student. It is about recognizing that innovation stems not from conformity but from the courage to chart our own path. So, let go of the fear of deviating from the norm, trust your instincts and creativity, and break the status quo.

There is no singular path to success, and genuine innovation often arises from embracing individuality and creativity. In today's rapidly changing educational landscape, it is crucial to recognize that what works for one educator, classroom, or school may not necessarily work for another. By acknowledging and celebrating the uniqueness of each educator, student, and learning environment, we open the door to a more inclusive approach to education. This means letting go of the fear of deviating from established norms and trusting in our instincts and creativity to guide us.

When educators dare to forge their paths and implement changes tailored to their specific contexts, it can spark transformation throughout the entire education system. Rather than adhering rigidly to convention, this willingness to innovate and adapt develops an environment where excellence can thrive. We can create a more dynamic, responsive, and effective education system by championing individuality and embracing evidence-based approaches to teaching and learning.

Let us paint a vivid picture of a personalized learning environment based on the examples in this book: places where students are empowered to take charge of their education. This transformative approach to education offers a glimpse into the possibilities and challenges you face to begin your journey, transforming your classroom or school in ways that unleash the potential of your learners.

Imagine a school brimming with enthusiastic students engaged in activities that pique their interests. In a media class, a group uses cameras to bring a music video to life. Nearby, another group constructs robots while others brainstorm ideas for a community project. Classrooms are transformed—rows of desks are replaced by collaborative tables where students can share knowledge and ideas. *In the art room, students delve into learning about Cyanotypes by choosing their preferred method—reading an article, listening to a podcast, or watching a video. Similarly, in the math classroom, technology allows students to progress at their own pace while the teacher provides individualized support.*

The science lab allows students to explore scientific concepts through inquiry and collaboration. They can choose from hands-on experiments, online simulations, or educational games to solidify their understanding. Classes can be tailored to meet students' varying needs, even within the same subject. In one ELA class, students select articles that pique their curiosity, while in another, some students participate in an online discussion while others receive individual feedback on their essays.

Teachers share laughter and camaraderie downstairs in the faculty room, reinforcing a sense of community and friendship. The principal visits classrooms, offering support and encouragement to both teachers and students. Through a blend of self-paced, project-based, and cross-curricular courses, students are empowered to take ownership of their education. Regular feedback facilitates growth and improvement, ensuring that every student learns.

Data is not just a buzzword but an enhancer of instruction. Daily formative assessments, benchmarks, and weekly data analysis sessions ensure continuous progress. Collaboration between teachers is critical, with weekly meetings and gatherings to spur continuous improvement. Beyond academics, a focus extends to empowering students with life skills. Mentorship programs and daily student prep periods nurture resilience, growth mindset, and social-emotional learning, preparing students for success beyond the classroom.

The journey towards personalized learning can serve as a catalyst for profound change, benefiting educators and students alike. Throughout this book, we have explored the what, why, and how of personalization in schools, equipping you with the knowledge and resources needed to embark on this path of innovation and growth.

As you stand at the precipice of change, it is your turn to seize the opportunity before you. Just like Mary shared at the start of this book, it's time to remove the shackles and move beyond traditional approaches. Embrace boldness, explore new techniques, and redefine your educational philosophy. Remember, there is no one-size-fits-all solution when it comes to personalized learning. You have been provided with the tools and resources to craft your dream school or classroom that celebrates diversity, instills creativity, and cultivates a love for learning.

The Spark Within

We have reached the final bend on this journey together. The book has explored the theoretical underpinnings of personalized learning, examined practical strategies, and witnessed the transformative power of this approach in real-world classrooms. Now comes the most crucial step – igniting the spark of personalized learning within your own educational environment.

Imagine classrooms alive with buzzing curiosity. Imagine students actively engaged, their passions fueling their learning progressions. This is not a utopian fantasy; it is the very essence of personalized learning. Personalization embodies nurturing the unique spark within each student, and instilling a love for learning that transcends textbooks and tests.

The Power Lies Within You: Not a Recipe, But a Canvas

This path is not about replicating a pre-made model or chasing a single solution that works for all students. Personalized learning is woven from your own creativity, commitment, and the unique fabric of your students. You are the architect, the designer, the champion. There is no script to follow, no rigid formula to enforce. Instead, personalized learning offers a canvas, a starting point for you to paint a vibrant picture of learning that resonates with each student.

Embrace Growth, Understand Your Learners

The foundation of personalized learning rests on a fundamental truth—every student can learn and grow. Ditch labels and preconceived notions. Embrace the potential within each individual and the dynamic nature of learning. This variation in perspective will fuel your passion and guide your approach. Understanding your students goes beyond grades and test scores. Dive deeper—observe their learning inclinations, interests, strengths, and challenges. Conduct surveys, hold regular student-led conferences, and create opportunities for self-reflection. Listen actively to their voices, their aspirations, and their anxieties. The more you know about your students, the more effectively you can personalize their learning experience.

Reimagine Curriculum, Technology as a Catalyst

Break down content into modular units, offering students choices and pathways that align with their interests and needs. Explore project-based learning, where students are immersed in real-world problems and collaborate to find solutions. Encourage student inquiry, allowing them to follow their curiosity and become active participants in their learning. Imagine a student passionate about marine biology diving deeper into ocean ecosystems. Personalized learning allows for focused exploration through virtual reality experiences or research projects on specific marine life.

Technology is a powerful tool for personalization, not a replacement for your expertise. Use it to differentiate instruction, offer flexible learning opportunities, and create engaging experiences. Consider adaptive learning platforms that personalize instruction. Online simulations can transport students to historical events or faraway lands, sparking curiosity and deeper understanding. Collaborative tools like digital whiteboards and online forums allow for real-time interaction and knowledge sharing among students.

> Remember, technology is a means to an end, not the end itself.

Remember, technology is a means to an end, not the end itself.

Assessment for Learning, Not Just of Learning

Gone are the days of standardized tests dictating the learning process. Personalized assessment focuses on understanding where each student is on their journey and what steps they need to take next. Use formative assessments such as observations, self-reflection journals, and student conferences to provide timely, personalized feedback that propels learning. Imagine a student struggling with a science concept. You can identify their specific challenges through personalized assessment and create targeted interventions, whether it's one-on-one instruction, peer tutoring, or curated online resources.

Collaboration and Communication are Key: Building a Network

You do not have to walk this path alone. Collaboration with colleagues is essential for success. Share ideas, resources, and strategies with fellow educators. Create professional learning communities dedicated to personalized learning, fostering a space for shared expertise and problem-solving. Seek out mentors who can offer guidance and support. Together, you can create a network of educators committed to transforming the learning experience for all students. Communication with students, parents, and the broader community is crucial. Share your vision for personalized learning, explain the "why" behind your strategies, and involve stakeholders in the process. Regular updates and open communication build trust, support collaboration for all, and garner valuable feedback to refine your approach.

Be the Change and Embrace Challenges

Personalized learning requires a shift in mindset from teacher-centered to student-centered. It is about empowering students to take ownership of their learning. Be a role model, demonstrating curiosity, a growth mindset, and a willingness to learn alongside your students. Let your passion for personalized learning be contagious. Encourage students to take risks and embrace mistakes as opportunities for growth. Create a safe space where students feel comfortable asking questions, exploring unique perspectives, and advocating for how they learn best.

The road to implementing personalized learning will not be entirely smooth. Expect bumps. There will be moments when frustration creeps in, and resources may seem limited. Remember, this is a process, not an event. Embrace challenges as opportunities for growth, refine your strategies, and keep the ultimate goal—igniting the spark within each student—in sight.

Celebrate the Journey, Your Legacy

Personalized learning is less about perfection and more about progress. Celebrate every milestone, every student success story, every "aha!" moment. Your commitment to personalized learning will inspire your students, colleagues, and community. Let your classroom be a catalyst for curiosity, engagement, and lifelong learning.

Remember, you hold the power to transform lives. By embracing personalized learning, you are not just shaping lessons; you are shaping learner success. The goal is to equip students with the skills, knowledge, competencies, and confidence they need to thrive in a world that demands adaptability, creativity, and a lifelong love of learning. Personalized learning is a journey, not a destination. Never lose sight of the potential you hold to ignite a lifelong love of learning in your students. Their futures and the future of education depend on it.

> By embracing personalized learning, you are not just shaping lessons; you are shaping learner success.

As you embark on this adventure, know that you are not alone. We believe in your ability to make a meaningful impact in the lives of your students and your community. So, step out with confidence, passion, and determination. Make a change today and let your vision for personalized learning inspire generations to come. You've got this.

References

Ainsworth, L. (2003). "Unwrapping" the standards: a simple process to make standards manageable. Englewood, CO: Advanced Learning Press.

Alsuwaiyan, H., & Alharbi, S. (2021). Exploring the impact of the 1:1 laptop initiative on students' academic achievement in Saudi Arabia. Journal of Educational Technology Development and Exchange (JETDE), 14(3), 85-97.

AlQahtani, M., & Alharbi, S. (2021). Investigating the impact of the 1:1 laptop program on students' self-motivation and engagement in learning in Saudi Arabia. International Journal of Instruction, 14(1), 385-402.

Amabile, T. M., & Kramer, S. J. (2011). The power of small wins. Harvard Business Review, 89(5), 70-80

Black, P., & Wiliam, D. (1998). Assessment and classroom learning. Assessment in Education: Principles, Policy & Practice, 5(1), 7–74.

Bloom, B. S. (1984). The two sigma problem: The search for methods of group instruction as effective as one-to-one tutoring. Educational Researcher, 13(6), 4–16.

Boekaerts, M., Pintrich, P. R., & Zeidner, M. (2000). Self-regulation in academic learning: Self-efficacy, enjoyment, and cognitive activation. Educational Psychologist, 35(4), 191–209.

Brooks, A. C., & Winfrey, O. (2023). The Art and Science of Getting Happier: Build the Life You Want. Portfolio Books.

Bry, B. M., & Schneider, B. (2002). Trust in schools: A critical review of the literature. Review of Educational Research, 72(3), 303-340.

Chen, S., & Wang, J. (2020). Individual differences and personalized learning: a review and appraisal. Universal Access in the Information Society, 20, 833-849.

Chen, W., & Zhang, M. (2020). Examining the impact of a 1:1 iPad initiative on student motivation and engagement in a middle school in China. Journal of Research in Innovative Teaching & Learning, 12(2), 149-163.

Cornelius-White, J. (2007). Learner-centered teacher-student relationships are effective: A meta-analysis. Review of Educational Research, 77(1), 113–143.

Deci, E. L., & Ryan, R. M. (2008). Self-determination theory: An overview of the theory and its applications. Human Development, 52(4), 331-360.

Devi, B., Khandelwal, B., & Das, M. (2017). Application of Bandura's social cognitive theory in the technology enhanced, blended learning environment. International Journal of Applied Research, 3(1), 721–724.

Dunlosky, J., Rawson, K. A., & Bjork, R. A. (2013. Explaining the benefits of self-explanations: A meta-analysis. Journal of Experimental Psychology: Learning, Memory, and Cognition, 39(4), 999–1022.

Ferguson, R. (2012). Learning analytics: drivers, developments, and challenges. International Journal of Technology Enhanced Learning, 4(5/6), 304–317.

Friend, M., Cook, L., Hurley-Chamberlain, D., & Shamberger, C. (2010). Co-Teaching: An Illustration of the Complexity of Collaboration in Special Education. Journal of Educational and Psychological Consultation, 20(1), 9-27.

Geier, D. (2019). The Best Leaders Are Skilled Communicators. Medium. Accessed at https://medium.com/the-helm/the-best-leaders-are-skilled-communicators-506c707ec8c8

Gregory, M. D., & Chapman, C. (2007. Differentiating literacy instruction in response to student readiness, interest, and learning profil.e. Reading Research Quarterly, 42(1), 37–60.

Hattie, J. (2009). Visible learning: A synthesis of over 800 meta-analyses relating to achievement. Corwin Press: Thousand Oaks, CA.

Hattie, J. (2012). Visible Learning for Teachers: Maximizing Impact on Learning. London: Routledge.

Hattie, J., & Timperley, H. (2007). The power of feedback. Review of Educational Research, 77(1), 81–112.

Hoyle, J. R., English, F. W., & Steffy, B. E. (1998). Skills for successful 21st-century school leaders: Standards for peak performers. Arlington, VA: American Association of School Administrators.

Hunter, M. C. (1994). "Enhancing teaching". New York, NY: Macmillan College Publishing Co.

Husmann, P.R., & V.D. O'Loughlin. (2019). "Another Nail in the Coffin for Learning Styles? Disparities among Undergraduate Anatomy Students' Study Strategies, Class Performance, and Reported Vark Learning Styles." Anatomical Sciences Education 12, 6–19.

Keller, H. (1903). *The Story of My Life*. New York, NY: Doubleday, Page & Company

Kirschner, P. 2017. "Stop Propagating the Learning Styles Myth." Computers and Education 106, 166–171.

Kulik, C. L. C., & Kulik, J. A. (1991). Effectiveness of computer-based instruction: An updated analysis. Computers in Human Behavior, 7(1-2), 75-94.

Lai, Y. Y., & Yuen, A. H. (2020). Exploring the effects of 1:1 laptop initiatives on student learning motivation and engagement. Education and Information Technologies, 25(5), 4113-4129.

Lee, M., & Choi, S. Y. (2022). The effects of 1:1 laptop programs on student achievement: A meta-analysis. Educational Technology Research and Development, 70(3), 1041-1062.

Leithwood, K., & Seashore Louis, K. (2010). Collective leadership in schools: Extending the conversation. Journal of Educational Administration, 48(8), 649-674.

Lieberman, A. (2007). Teachers and educational research: The missing agenda. Educational Researcher, 36(7), 3-10.

Locke, E. A., & Latham, G. P. (2002). Building a practically useful theory of goal setting and task motivation: A 35-year journey. American Psychologist, 57(9), 705-732.

London, M., & Smither, J. W. (2002). Feedback orientation, feedback culture, and the longitudinal performance management process. Human Resource Management Review, 12(1), 81-100.

Marzano, R. J. (2003). What Works in Schools: Translating Research into Action. Association for Supervision and Curriculum Development: Alexandria, VA.

Mason, V. (2021). Teach up: Empowering educators through cultural responsiveness, relationships, relevance. Houghton Mifflin Harcourt: Boston, MA.

Massa, L. J., & Mayer, R. E. (2006). Testing the ATI hypothesis: Should multimedia instruction accommodate verbalizer-visualizer cognitive style? Learning and Individual Differences, 16(4), 321–335.

Mazur, M. (2019). 3 Word Rebellion: Create a one-of-a-kind message that grows your business into a movement. Communication Rebel.

Means, B., Toyama, Y., Murphy, R., Bakia, M., & Jones, K. (2009). Evaluation of evidence-based practices in online learning: A meta-analysis and review of online learning studies. U.S. Department of Education, Office of Planning, Evaluation, and Policy Development.

Means, B., Toyama, Y., Murphy, R., & Baki, M. (2013). The effectiveness of online and blended learning: A meta-analysis of the empirical literature. Teachers College Record, 115(3), 1-47.

Moss, C. M., & Brookhart, S. M. (2001). Learning by doing: Evaluating student learning for understanding. Educational Leadership, 58(8), 30-32.

Murawski, W. W., & Swanson, H. L. (2001). A Meta-Analysis of Co-Teaching Research: Where Are the Data? Remedial and Special Education, 22(5), 258-267.

Murillo-Zamorano, S., Suárez-Guerrero, C., & Martínez-Garzón, M. (2020). Influence of computers in students' academic achievement: A systematic review. Journal of Educational Technology Development and Exchange (JETDE), 13(3), 33-49.

Niess, M. L., & Gillow-Wiles, H. (Eds.). (2021). Handbook of research on transforming teachers' online pedagogical reasoning for teaching K-12 students in virtual learning environments. IGI Global.

Osterman, K. F. (2000). Students' need for belonging in the school community. Review of Educational Research, 70(3), 323-367.

Pashler, H., McDaniel, M., Rohrer, D., & Bjork, R. (2008). Learning Styles: Concepts and Evidence. Psychological Science in the Public Interest, 9(3), 105-119.

Pianta, R. C. (1999). Enhancing relationships between children and teachers. American Psychologist, 91(1), 6-28.

Popham, W. J. (2008). The truth about testing: An educator's call to action. Association for Supervision and Curriculum Development: Alexandria, VA.

Puentedura, R. (2010). SAMR: A contextualized introduction. Retrieved from http://www.hippasus.com/rrpweblog/

Riener, C., and D.T. Willingham, 2010. "The Myth of Learning Styles." Change: The Magazine of Higher Learning 42(5), 32–35.

Robinson, J. D., & Persky, A. M. (2020). Developing Self-Directed Learners. American journal of pharmaceutical education, 84(3), 847512.

Roorda, D. L., Koomen, H. M. Y., Spilt, J. L., & Oort, F. J. (2011). The influence of affective teacher-student relationships on students' school engagement and achievement: A meta-analytic approach. Review of Educational Research, 81(4), 493-529.

Scruggs, T. E., Mastropieri, M. A., & McDuffie, K. A. (2007). Co-Teaching in Inclusive Classrooms: A Metasynthesis of Qualitative Research. Exceptional Children, 73(4), 392-416.

Shemshack, A., , K., & Spector, J. (2021). A comprehensive analysis of personalized learning components. Journal of Computers in Education, 8, 485 - 503.

Sheninger, E. (2021). Disruptive Thinking in Our Classrooms: Preparing Learners for Their Future. ConnectEDD Publishing: Chicago, IL

Sheninger, E. (2015). Uncommon Learning. Corwin: Thousand Oaks, CA

Sheninger, E. & Murray, T. (2017). Learning Transformed: 8 Keys to Designing Tomorrow's Schools, Today. ASCD: Alexandria, VA

Sheninger, E., & Rubin, T. (2017). BrandED: Tell your story, build relationships, empower learning. San Francisco, CA: Jossey-Bass.

Tetzlaff, L., Schmiedek, F., & Brod, G. (2020). Developing Personalized Education: A Dynamic Framework. Educational Psychology Review, 33, 863 - 882.

Vaughn, M. (2021). Student Agency in the Classroom: Honoring Student Voice in the Curriculum. Teachers College Press.

Vygotsky, L. S. (1978). Mind in society: The development of higher psychological processes. Harvard University Press.

Walsh, J. M., & Jones, B. (2019). Collaborative Teaching: Advantages and Challenges for Teachers and Students. Journal of Education and Training Studies, 7(11), 20-30.

Wen, Z., Sparks, R., Biedroń, A. & Teng, M. (2023). Cognitive Individual Differences in Second Language Acquisition: Theories, Assessment and Pedagogy. Berlin, Boston: De Gruyter Mouton.

Wiggins, G., & McTighe, J. (2005) Understanding by design (2nd ed.). Alexandria, VA: Association for Supervision and Curriculum Development ASCD.

Appendices

Here you will find an array of resources to help you personalize in your classroom, school, district, or organization. It is in a digital format so that new resources can easily be added and anything that is irrelevant removed.

Appendix 1: Digital tools to help personalize instruction and pedagogy, including artificial intelligence **bit.ly/PLbook_edtech**

Appendix 2: K-12 examples of high-agency practices (voice, choice, path, pace, and place) **bit.ly/PLbook_agency**

Appendix 3: K-12 rubric examples **bit.ly/PLbook_rubrics**

Appendix 4: Station rotation examples across various grade levels and content areas **bit.ly/PLbook_rotations**

Appendix 5: High-definition images found throughout the book in color **bit.ly/PLbook_images**

About the Authors

Eric Sheninger works with schools throughout the world, helping educators meet and exceed their potential to improve outcomes for learners. He is the founder and CEO of Aspire Change EDU, a collaborative consultancy designed to provide personalized support to all educational systems. Prior to this, he was a teacher and award-winning Principal at New Milford High School. Under his leadership, his school became a globally recognized model for innovative practices. Eric oversaw the successful implementation of several sustainable change initiatives that radically transformed the learning culture at his school while increasing achievement.

His work focuses on empowering educators to unlock the potential in all learners as well as themselves. Eric has emerged as an innovative leader, best-selling author, and sought-after speaker. Eric has received numerous awards and acknowledgments for his work. He is a Center for Digital Education Top 30 Award recipient, Bammy Award winner, National Association for Secondary School Principals Digital Principal Award winner, Phi Delta Kappa Emerging Leader Award recipient, winner of Learning Forward's Excellence in Professional Practice Award, Google Certified Innovator, Adobe Education Leader, and Association for Supervision and Curriculum Development 2011 Conference Scholar. He has authored or co-authored eight books, including *Disruptive Thinking in Our Classrooms* and *Digital Leadership*.

Eric began his career in education as a science teacher at Watchung Hills Regional High School in Warren, New Jersey. He then transitioned into the field of educational administration, first as an athletic director and supervisor of physical education and health and then as vice principal in the New Milford School District. Eric earned a Bachelor of Science degree from Salisbury University, a Bachelor of Science from the University of Maryland Eastern Shore, and a Master of Education in educational administration from East Stroudsburg University. Connect with Eric at: ericsheninger.com, esheninger@gmail.com, or follow @E_Sheninger on Twitter.

Nicki Slaugh stands out as a trailblazer in the field of educational transformation. Through her efforts, she has established a school culture dedicated to customizing learning experiences for individual students, cultivating a positive atmosphere, highlighting the importance of STEM education, and purposefully integrating technology to unleash each student's potential. As a secondary principal, Nicki's forward-thinking leadership has transformed a conventionally structured school into one that advocates for personalized, competency-based learning, attracting nationwide attention.

Nicki's focus has been creating proficiency scales, developing rubrics, self-paced pathways, incorporating technology as a resource, and giving teachers and students voice and choice in the classroom. Nicki is a Google-certified innovator who is certified in Magic-SchoolAI. Notable achievements include creating a Mastery Tracker for students and enhancing student progress in competency-based learning environments. Additionally, Nicki has presented her work at numerous local and national conferences teaching educators and leaders. Nicki championed innovative practices and received the Teacher of the Year Award, Model School Award, and was part of the reason her school accomplished being one of the first STEM-designated schools in Utah. Slaugh served as the Ogden/Weber Partners in Education Chair for three years, where she facilitated collaborative efforts to enhance educational opportunities for students.

Nicki Slaugh's education legacy spans over two decades, starting as a classroom teacher from kindergarten to third grade. She also served as an instructional technology and curriculum coach for grades K-9. Nicki currently serves as a secondary principal, fueled by a passionate commitment to cultivating a love of learning within her school. Nicki has a Bachelor's in Early Childhood, a Master's in Educational Leadership, Gifted and Talented Endorsement, and an Administrative License. Connect with Nicki at: slaughnicki@gmail.com

principal_nickislaugh (IG)
@nickiatquest (X)
nickislaugh.com

More from ConnectEDD Publishing

Since 2015, ConnectEDD has worked to transform education by empowering educators to become better-equipped to teach, learn, and lead. What started as a small company designed to provide professional learning events for educators has grown to include a variety of services to help educators and administrators address essential challenges. ConnectEDD offers instructional and leadership coaching, professional development workshops focusing on a variety of educational topics, a roster of nationally recognized educator associates who possess hands-on knowledge and experience, educational conferences custom-designed to meet the specific needs of schools, districts, and state/national organizations, and ongoing, personalized support, both virtually and onsite. In 2020, ConnectEDD expanded to include publishing services designed to provide busy educators with books and resources consisting of practical information on a wide variety of teaching, learning, and leadership topics. Please visit us online at connecteddpublishing.com or contact us at: info@connecteddpublishing.com

Recent Publications:

Disruptive Thinking: Preparing Learners for Their Future by Eric Sheninger

Live Your Excellence: Action Guide by Jimmy Casas

Culturize: Action Guide by Jimmy Casas

Daily Inspiration for Educators: Positive Thoughts for Every Day of the Year by Jimmy Casas

Eyes on Culture: Multiply Excellence in Your School by Emily Paschall

Pause. Breathe. Flourish. Living Your Best Life as an Educator by William D. Parker

L.E.A.R.N.E.R. Finding the True, Good, and Beautiful in Education by Marita Diffenbaugh

Educator Reflection Tips Volume II: Refining Our Practice by Jami Fowler-White

Handle With Care: Managing Difficult Situations in Schools with Dignity and Respect by Jimmy Casas and Joy Kelly

Permission to be Great: Increasing Engagement in Your School by Dan Butler

Daily Inspiration for Educators: Positive Thoughts for Every Day of the Year. Volume II by Jimmy Casas

The 6 Literacy Levers: Creating a Community of Readers by Brad Gustafson

The Educator's ATLAS: Your Roadmap to Engagement by Weston Kieschnick

In This Season: Words for the Heart by Todd Nesloney, LaNesha Tabb, Tanner Olson, and Alice Lee

Leading with a Humble Heart: A 40-Day Devotional for Leaders by Zac Bauermaster

Recalibrate the Culture: Our Why…Our Work…Our Values by Jimmy Casas

Creating Curious Classrooms: The Beauty of Questions by Emma Chiappetta

Crafting the Culture: 45 Reflections on What Matters Most by Joe Sanfelippo and Jeffrey Zoul

Improving School Mental Health: The Thriving School Community Solution by Charle Peck and Dr. Cameron Caswell

Building Authenticity: A Blueprint for the Leader Inside You by Todd Nesloney And Tyler Cook

Connecting Through Conversation: A Playbook for Talking with Kids by Erika Bare and Tiffany Burns

The Dream Factory: Designing a Purposeful Life by Mark Trumbo

Stories Behind Stances: Creating Empathy Through Hearing "The Other Side" by Chris Singleton

Happy Eyes: All Things to All People by Ryan Tillman

The Generative Age Artificial Intelligence and the Future of Education by Alana Winnick

Recalibrate the Culture: Action Guide by Jimmy Casas

Leading with PEOPLE: A Six Pillar Framework for Fruitful Leadership by Zac Bauermaster

A School Leader's Guide to Reclaiming Purpose by Frederick C. Buskey

Foundations of an Elite Culture: Building Success with High Standards and a Positive Environment by David Arencibia

www.ingramcontent.com/pod-product-compliance
Lightning Source LLC
Chambersburg PA
CBHW070702130626
46553CB00005B/1806

* 9 7 9 8 9 8 9 0 0 2 7 3 3 *